EXETER MEDIEVAL ENGLISH TEXTS AND STUDIES
General Editors: Marion Glasscoe & M.J. Swanton

The Crucifixion, from an English Missal of 1461
Bodleian Library, MS. Digby 227, f. 113ᵛ

English Medieval Religious Lyrics

Edited

by

DOUGLAS GRAY

UNIVERSITY
of
EXETER
PRESS

Reprinted by arrangement with Oxford University Press
© Oxford University Press, 1975

This revised edition
University of Exeter Press, 1992
Reed Hall
Streatham Drive
Exeter EX4 4QR
UK

www.exeterpress.co.uk

Printed digitally since 2010

British Library Cataloguing in Publication Data
A catalogue record for this book
is available from the British Library

ISBN 978 0 85989 382 4

CONTENTS

CONTENTS

INTRODUCTION

ONE of England's most remarkable contributions to medieval literature is a large body of religious lyric verse. The poems appear in profusion in manuscripts of the thirteenth to the early sixteenth centuries, and far outnumber the secular lyrics that have survived (though these no doubt were less likely to be recorded by pious copyists). They are the product of a living native tradition of piety and devotional writing, which can be traced back to pre-Conquest times. The Old English religious poets did not (so it seems from the surviving evidence) use the characteristic forms of the later lyrics, but in such poems as *The Dream of the Rood* and *Christ* as well as in some homilies there are distinct hints of the passionate devotion so notable in the Middle Ages. In the century after the Conquest there are echoes of Anglo-Saxon spirituality, especially in the eremitical tradition (a number of the hermits from this time have Saxon, not French names—Sigar, Godric, etc.; in the Latin life of the twelfth-century recluse Christina of Markyate her spiritual director calls her in homely English 'myn sunendaege dohter'). Godric, the hermit of Finchale (d. 1170), is said to have been taught by the Virgin Mary 'canticum quoddam novum'; his English version sounds like the simple vernacular prayers of the type so frequently found in later centuries:

> Sainte Marie Virgine,
> Moder Jesu Cristes Nazarene,
> Onfo, schild, help thin Godric;
> Onfang, bring heghilich with the in Godes riche.[1]

Much later, in a book on the solitary life, a Carthusian, Richard de Methley (d. 1528), recalls the incident and the hymn for his reader, 'Hugh hermit': 'and when thou sittest by thy oon in the wilderness and art weak or weary, say this to our Lady, as

---

[1] *Index* 2988; J. Hall, *Selections from Early Middle English* (Oxford, 1920), i, p. 5.

S. Godric said, that holy hermit: *Sancta Maria, virgo* . . . He said *adjuva tuum Godricum*, but thou may say, *tuum Hugonem*, for thy name is Hugh' (thus losing the gentle pun which the saint made on his own name). Because of the social and cultural changes and the religious turmoil that followed Methley's time the medieval English pious lyrics faded and declined, but they bequeathed much of their spirit as well as a number of traditional images and phrases to later poets.

Not surprisingly, the huge corpus of devotional lyric contains much that is uninspired and hackneyed, concerning which one might well echo Johnson's judgement of Watts's verse, that 'the paucity of its topicks enforces perpetual repetition'. But the best of the lyrics show a remarkable freshness and variety. Even the verses on death, which superficially seem a very homogeneous group, reveal subtle modulations of tone and mood: some are bleak and austere statements of the contempt of the world; some are grimly, or grotesquely, macabre; others express more gentle emotions in a more dignified tone, and one (No. 83) suggests a sceptical and questioning mind. The song of moral instruction may become the vehicle of a satire which is sharp and uncompromising, or openly comic (No. 78). We find the same variety in form and structure. The lyrics may be simple, ejaculatory prayers, or memorable snatches, or songs, or (perhaps most characteristically) reflective or meditative poems, often of some length. Some have a simple narrative structure, others are dramatic scenes, or sustained dramatic monologues. We may find the plainest couplets or quatrains, or elaborately patterned stanzas, and imitations of the forms of contemporary courtly verse.

The religious lyrics were part of the practical piety of the time—'for a more devout prayere fond I never of the passioun, who so wolde devoutly say hitte' the rubric of one remarks approvingly.[1] They were written to be used, and used they were, sometimes in sermons, sometimes for display as inscriptions, sometimes for private prayer or meditation. We should not therefore expect to find our attention directed to the inner

[1] *CB XIV*, p. 114.

life of the individual poets who created them. Whether a poet uses the word 'I' or 'we' in addressing his audience, he means his readers to join with him in devotion. Even when an eminent poet, such as Chaucer, of whose creative individuality there is no question, writes a religious lyric he will adopt the traditional self-effacing manner.

Simplicity and unaffectedness are the characteristic features of the style. Paradox and word-play are not avoided, and verbal decoration is by no means totally absent—in the fifteenth century some poems (especially those which celebrate the Assumption and the Coronation of the Virgin) are adorned with the golden or 'aureate' vocabulary which was made popular by Lydgate (cf. especially Dunbar's 'Hale, sterne superne').[1] The majority, however, either avoid self-conscious or complex figurative expressions altogether, or are content with traditional metaphors and images. This can be quickly illustrated by setting some lines from one of our poems (No. 12):

> For in this rose conteynyd was
> Heven and erthe in lytyl space
> *Res miranda*

against Donne's later statement of the same idea:

> Yea, thou art now
> Thy Makers maker, and thy Fathers mother,
> Thou hast light in darke, and shutst in little roome,
> Immensity cloisterd in thy deare wombe.

The notion that 'plain words reach the heart' was a commonplace of medieval devotional rhetoric:

> Planus sermo usque ad cor penetrat;
> Politus autem pascit aures.
> Playn word entereth the hert;
> Iflarysched the eeres feedyt.[2]

---

[1] William Dunbar, *Poems*, ed. J. Kinsley (Oxford, 1958), No. 4.
[2] *Index* 2757; R. H. Robbins, *Secular Lyrics of the XIVth and XVth Centuries* (Oxford, 1952), p. l.

The lyrics are full of homely and often vivid words and phrases from ordinary speech ('bobbid', 'bereth the belle', 'fowre thowsand wynter thowt he not to long', 'Ur bagge hongeth on a sliper pyn', etc.) or proverbial expressions ('The tide abidith no man', 'Here today awey tomorn', etc.)—a characteristic which they share with longer religious poems, such as *Piers Plowman*, and, for all its artifice, *Pearl*. Of the devotional lyric we may say as Joan Evans does of the English art of the period that 'its charm lies in its naturalness and a touching kind of simplicity'.

The English religious lyric was by no means an isolated or an insular phenomenon, however. It was deeply indebted to the common Western European Christian tradition of which it was part. From the Bible, the Psalter, the liturgy, and from innumerable Latin hymns, poems, and meditations the poets took phrases, images, and ideas. Sometimes a whole poem is translated from a Latin hymn (e.g. No. 75), or based on a part of the liturgy (e.g. No. 29). The best lyrics use this traditional material with subtlety, and make of it something fresh and individual—cf. the triumphant ring of the vigorous English version of *Aurora lucis rutilat* (No. 38), or the way in which a few lines of St. Augustine become, in isolation, a moving penitential verse (No. 79 (b)).

The devotional attitudes of the lyrics are those of the central tradition of European piety in the Middle Ages. They are inspired by that fervent devotion especially addressed to the persons of Christ and his mother, which in its intense contemplation of the mystery of man's redemption stresses that 'love was our Lord's meaning', a devotional tradition which is particularly associated with the names of Anselm, Bernard of Clairvaux, and Francis of Assisi. This 'style' of devotion was spread by the new preaching orders of the thirteenth century (the Franciscans especially played an important part in the development of the religious lyric and carol in England, and provide two of the named authors—Herebert and Ryman—represented in this selection); it is worth recalling that it is characteristic also of the older tradition of the eremitical and solitary life, represented in the

Middle Ages by individual hermits like Richard Rolle, or by austere orders like the Carthusians (who in England in the later Middle Ages were notable collectors of devotional and mystical books).

Many of the English lyrics have the intimate tenderness and pathos which are characteristic of the best works produced by this tradition. A tough realism, a sense of man's inadequacy, a precise and delicate use of language save them from the emotionalism and cloying sweetness into which affective devotion may degenerate. The best of them avoid the dangers, on the one hand of an arid formalism, and on the other of an unrestrained popular enthusiasm, to achieve a remarkable dignity, moderation, and clarity. They have a quality which is best described by the phrase of Julian of Norwich, a 'marvellous homeliness':

> For love of Jesu, my swete herte,
> Y morne and seke wyth teres smert.[1]

This *Selection* presents a number of the more attractive and interesting of the religious lyrics. It has been thought best to exclude lyrics by known authors who have volumes in this series devoted to their work (such as Lydgate, and in particular Dunbar, several of whose religious lyrics are among the masterpieces of the tradition). It was originally intended also to exclude carols, which are handsomely represented in R. L. Greene's *Selection of English Carols* in this series. However, since that volume is now unobtainable, a few carols have been added.

The poems are not arranged chronologically, but according to the subject-matter, roughly forming a 'Scheme of Redemption' from the Fall of man to the Last Things and the hope of heaven. Some of the many 'snatches'—short prayers, sermon tags, couplets, etc.—are used as headpieces to introduce the various groups of lyrics.

In the texts, þ, ð, ʒ are transliterated into their modern equivalents, initial *ff* is represented by *F*, *u/v* and *i/j* are standardized

[1] *Index* 834; Carleton Brown, *A Register of ME Religious Verse* (Oxford, 1920), i, p. 131.

according to modern usage. Scribal abbreviations are expanded. One or two other spellings which might puzzle modern readers have been changed: silent *h* (*hic* for *ic*) has been removed, *h* has been restored initially in forms like *is* = *his*, the form of the 2 sg.pers.pron. has been standardized as *thou*, forms of Jesu(s) have been standardized, *th* spellings in forms like *mith* have been represented as *ht*. Punctuation is editorial.

I am grateful to a number of libraries for allowing me to consult manuscript material, notably to the Bodleian Library; the British Museum; the Cambridge University Library; Lambeth Palace Library; the National Library of Scotland; the Victoria and Albert Museum; Durham Cathedral Library; Durham University Library; The Huntington Library; Ushaw College, Durham; University, Magdalen, Merton, Balliol, New, and Corpus Christi Colleges, Oxford; Trinity College, Cambridge; the Fitzwilliam Museum, the Pepys Library, and Magdalene College, Cambridge. I am also grateful to Mrs. Felicity J. Riddy of the University of Stirling who allowed me to make use of her unpublished thesis. I have much pleasure in acknowledging helpful advice from Professor N. Davis and Miss C. Sisam, and, most of all, the constant encouragement and criticism of Professor J. A. W. Bennett, the General Editor of the series.

The frontispiece (reproduced by courtesy of the Curators of the Bodleian Library) shows a forceful, if not very elegant, English treatment of the crucifixion from the late Middle Ages. The Missal (1461) was made for Abingdon Abbey (the arms at the foot are those of the abbey and of Abbot William Ashenden); it was illuminated by William Abell (see O. Pächt and J. J. G. Alexander, *Illuminated MSS. in the Bodleian Library*, iii (Oxford, 1973), No. 1065, M. Rickert, *Painting in Britain. The Middle Ages* (Harmondsworth, 1965), pp. 185, 249 n. 9).

SELECT BIBLIOGRAPHY

(with abbreviations used in this volume)

I. TEXTS

Anthologies

Carleton Brown, *English Lyrics of the XIIIth Century* (Oxford, 1932) [CB XIII]
—— *Religious Lyrics of the XIVth Century* (rev. G. V. Smithers, Oxford, 1952) [CB XIV]
—— *Religious Lyrics of the XVth Century* (Oxford, 1939) [CB XV]
E. K. Chambers and F. Sidgwick, *Early English Lyrics* (London, 1921) [EEL]
R. T. Davies, *Medieval English Lyrics* (London, 1963) [Davies]
R. L. Greene, *Early English Carols* (Oxford, 1935) [EEC]
—— *A Selection of English Carols* (Oxford, 1962) [Greene, Sel.]
H. A. Person, *Cambridge ME Lyrics* (Seattle, 1953) [Person]
T. Silverstein, *Medieval English Lyrics* (London, 1971)
C. and K. Sisam, *The Oxford Book of Medieval English Verse* (Oxford, 1970) [Sisam]
J. Stevens, *Medieval Carols* (*Musica Britannica* iv, London, 1952).

Some editions and studies of individual MS. collections or categories of lyrics

J. A. W. Bennett, *Devotional Pieces in Verse and Prose* (STS 3rd ser. xxiii (1949)) (MS. Arundel 285)
G. L. Brook, *The Harley Lyrics* (Manchester, 1948)
R. Dyboski, *Songs, Carols, and other Miscellaneous Poems* (EETS, ES ci (1907)) (MS. Balliol 354)
W. Heuser, *Die Kildare-Gedichte* (*Bonner Beiträge zur Anglistik*, xiv, Bonn, 1904) (MS. Harley 913)
N. R. Ker, *Facsimile of B.M. MS. Harley 2253* (EETS cclv (1965))
K. Reichl, *Religiöse Dichtung im englischen Hochmittelalter* (Munich, 1973) (MS. Trin. Coll., Camb., 323) [Reichl]

A. G. Rigg, *A Glastonbury Miscellany of the XVth Century* (Oxford, 1968) (MS. Trin. Coll., Camb., 1450) [Rigg]

R. H. Robbins, 'The Arma Christi Rolls', *MLR* xxxiv (1939), 415–21

—— 'The Gurney Series of Religious Lyrics', *PMLA*, liv (1939), 369–90

—— 'ME Verse Levation Prayers', *MP* xl (1942), 131–46

—— 'Popular Prayers in ME Verse', *MP* xxxvi (1939), 337–50

—— 'Private Prayers in ME Verse', *SP* xxxvi (1939), 466–75

—— 'Signs of Death in ME', *Medieval Studies* xxxii (1970), 282–98

H. E. Sandison, *The 'Chanson d'Aventure' in Middle English* (Bryn Mawr, Pa., 1913) [Sandison]

Edward Wilson, *A Descriptive Index of the English Lyrics in John of Grimestone's Preaching Book* (Medium Ævum Monographs, N.S. ii (Oxford, 1973)) (MS. Advocates 18.7.21) [Wilson]

T. Wright, *Songs and Carols* (Warton Club iv, London, 1856) (MS. Sloane 2593)

II. CRITICAL STUDIES

V. Gillespie, 'Mystic's Foot: Rolle and Affectivity', *The Medieval Mystical Tradition in England*, ii, ed. Marion Glasscoe (Exeter, 1982), 199–230

D. Gray, *Themes and Images in the Medieval English Religious Lyric* (London, 1972)

G. Kane, *Middle English Literature* (London, 1951) (ch. ii)

S. Manning, *Wisdom and Number* (Lincoln, Nebr., 1962)

R. Oliver, *Poems Without Names* (Berkeley, Calif., 1970)

F. A. Patterson, *The Middle English Penitential Lyric* (New York, 1911)

Edmund Reiss, *The Art of the Middle English Lyric* (Athens, Ga., 1972)

R. H. Robbins, 'The Authors of the ME Religious Lyrics', *JEGP* xxxix (1940), 230–8

—— 'The Earliest Carols and the Franciscans', *MLN* liii (1938), 239–45.

W. E. Rogers, *Image and Abstraction. Six Middle English Religious Lyrics* (*Anglistica*, xviii (Copenhagen, 1972))

R. D. Stevick, 'The Criticism of ME Lyrics', *MP* lxiv (1966), 103–17

S. A. Weber, *Theology and Poetry in the Middle English Lyric* (Columbus, Ohio, 1969)

S. Wenzel, *Preachers, Poets, and the Early English Lyric* (Princeton, N.J., 1986)

T. Wolpers, 'Geschichte der englischen Marienlyrik im Mittelalter', *Anglia* lxix (1950), 3–88

T. Wolpers, 'Zum Andachtsbild in der mittelenglischen religiösen Lyrik' in *Chaucer und seine Zeit. Symposion für Walter Schirmer*, ed. A. Esch Tübingen, 1968), pp. 293–336

Rosemary Woolf, *The English Religious Lyric in the Middle Ages* (Oxford, 1968) [Woolf]

III. OTHER USEFUL WORKS

Erich Auerbach, *Mimesis* (Bern, 1946; tr. W. R. Trask, Princeton, 1953)

H. Brinkmann, 'Voraussetzungen und Struktur religiöser Lyrik im Mittelalter', *Mittellateinisches Jahrbuch* iii (1966), 37–54

J. E. Colledge, *The Medieval Mystics of England* (London, 1962) (intro.)

E. R. Curtius, *Europäische Literatur und lateinisches Mittelalter* (Bern, 1948), tr. W. R. Trask, *European Literature and the Latin Middle Ages* (London, 1953)

Peter Dronke, *The Medieval Lyric* (London, 1968)

L. Gougaud, *Dévotions et pratiques ascétiques du moyen âge* (Paris, 1925)

J. Huizinga, *The Waning of the Middle Ages* (English ed., London, 1924)

V. A. Kolve, *The Play called Corpus Christi* (London, 1966) [Kolve]

J. Leclercq, F. Vandenbroucke, L. Bouyer, *The Spirituality of the Middle Ages* (tr. the Benedictines of Holme Eden, London, 1968)

G. Leff, *Medieval Thought. St. Augustine to Ockham* (London, 1958)

L. L. Martz, *The Poetry of Meditation* (rev. ed. New Haven, Conn., 1962)

G. R. Owst, *Literature and Pulpit in Medieval England* (1st ed. Cambridge, 1933; revised ed. Oxford, 1961)

—— *Preaching in Medieval England* (Cambridge, 1926)

W. A. Pantin, *The English Church in the Fourteenth Century* (Cambridge, 1955)

F. J. E. Raby, *Christian Latin Poetry* (Oxford, 1953)

SELECT BIBLIOGRAPHY

B. Smalley, *English Friars and Antiquity in the Fourteenth Century* (Oxford, 1960)

—— *The Study of the Bible in the Middle Ages* (2nd ed. Oxford, 1952)

R. W. Southern, *Western Society and the Church in the Middle Ages* (Harmondsworth, 1970)

J. Szövérffy, *Die Annalen der lateinischer Hymnendichtung* (Berlin, 1964–5), 2 vols.

Rosemond Tuve, *A Reading of George Herbert* (London, 1952)

J. Walsh (ed.), *Pre-Reformation English Spirituality* (London, 1966)

B. J. Whiting, *Proverbs, Sentences and Proverbial Phrases from English Writings mainly before 1500* (Cambridge, Mass., 1968) [Whiting]

A. Wilmart, *Auteurs spirituels et textes dévots du moyen âge latin* (Paris, 1932)

OTHER ABBREVIATIONS USED

Archiv	*Archiv für das Studium neueren Sprachen*
B.M.	British Museum
Bodl.	Bodleian Library
C.U.L.	Cambridge University Library
Daniel, *Thes.*	H. A. Daniel, *Thesaurus hymnologicus* (Halle, Leipzig, 1841–56), 5 vols.
Dreves	*Analecta Hymnica*, ed. G. M. Dreves (and C. Blume) (Leipzig, 1886–), 54 vols.
EETS	Early English Text Society (ES: Extra Series)
EGS	*English and Germanic Studies*
ELH	*Journal of English Literary History*
HLQ	*Huntington Library Quarterly*
Index	Carleton Brown and R. H. Robbins, *The Index of Middle English Verse* (N.Y., 1943), *Supplement* by R. H. Robbins and J. L. Cutler (Lexington, Ky., 1965)
JEGP	*Journal of English and Germanic Philology*
MÆ	*Medium Ævum*
ME	Middle English
MED	*Middle English Dictionary*, ed. H. Kurath and S. M. Kuhn (Ann Arbor, 1956–)
MLN	*Modern Language Notes*
MLR	*Modern Language Review*
Mone	F. J. Mone, *Lateinische Hymnen des Mittelalters* (Freiburg, 1853–5), 3 vols.
MP	*Modern Philology*
N.L.S.	National Library of Scotland
NM	*Neuphilologische Mitteilungen*
NQ	*Notes and Queries*
OBMLV	*The Oxford Book of Medieval Latin Verse*, ed. F. J. E. Raby (Oxford, 1959)
OE	Old English

OED	*The Oxford English Dictionary*
PL	*Patrologia Latina*, ed. J. P. Migne (Paris, 1844–), 221 vols.
PMLA	*Publications of the Modern Language Association*
PPl	*Piers Plowman*
RES	*Review of English Studies*
RF	Robbins Festschrift: *Chaucer and Middle English Studies in honour of Rossell Hope Robbins*, ed. B. Rowland (London, 1974)
SP	*Studies in Philology*
STC	*Short-Title Catalogue of English Books, 1475–1640*, ed. A. W. Pollard and G. R. Redgrave (London, 1926)
STS	Scottish Text Society
Vg	Vulgate

LIST OF MANUSCRIPTS AND LOCATIONS

THIS checklist contains MSS. from which texts in the selection are taken, MSS. mentioned in the critical apparatus, and the most important of those referred to in the notes. The note to each poem gives a reference to its entry in the *Index of Middle English Verse*, where further bibliographical information can be obtained.

I. LONDON

(a) British Museum

Add. MS. 22283 ('Simeon' MS.) (No. 83)
Add. MS. 34193 (No. 75)
Add. MS. 37049 (No. 46(b))
Add. MS. 46919 (Nos. 29, 37(a), 40)
Arundel 285 (Nos. 39, 62)
Arundel 286 (No. 35)
Cotton Caligula A. II (No. 60)
Cotton Faustina B. VI, Pt. II (No. 88)
Egerton 613 (No. 7)
Egerton 615
Egerton 1995 (No. 86(b))
'Fayrfax' MS. (= Add. MS. 5465)
Harley 211 (No. 50(a))
Harley 665 (No. 8(a))

Harley 667 (No. 67)
Harley 913 (No. 82)
Harley 2251
Harley 2253 (No. 86(a))
Harley 2316 (Nos. 28, 81)
Harley 4012 (No. 27)
Harley 5398 (No. 77(a))
Harley 7322 (Nos. 4(a), 14, 87)
Harley 7358
Harley Charter 58 C. 14
Lansdowne 762
Royal 8. F. II
Royal 9. C. II (No. 91)
Royal 12. E. I (Nos. 23, 33)
Sloane 2593 (Nos. 2, 6, 13)
Stowe 39

(b) Lambeth Palace Library

Lambeth 78
Lambeth 557 (No. 41)

Lambeth 853 (No. 63)

(c) Victoria and Albert Museum

Dyce 45 (No. 42)   Reid 7 (No. 65)

II. OXFORD

(a) Bodleian Library

Arch. Selden B 26 (No. 9)
Arch. Selden supra 74 (No. 21)
Ashmole 176
Ashmole 1393
Bodley 26 (Nos. 1(*a*), 1(*b*))
Bodley 416 (No. 30)
Bodley 649
Bodley 789 (No. 54)
Bodley 791 (No. 17)
Digby 2 (No. 32)
Digby 86 (Nos. 48, 53(*e*))
Don. C. 13 (No. 49)
Douce 78
Douce 104 (No. 78)
Douce 295 (No. 34)

Douce 322 (No. 61)
e Mus. 23 (No. 58)
Eng. poet. e 1 (Nos. 10, 76)
Laud misc. 23 (No. 85)
Laud misc. 108 (No. 71)
Laud misc. 213 (No. 77(*b*))
Lyell 24
Lyell 30 (Nos. 53(*a*), (*c*), 64)
Rawl. B. 332 (No. 72)
Rawl. C. 86
Rawl. liturg. f. 36 (No. 53(*b*))
Rawl. poet. 34 (No. 57)
Tanner 407
Vernon MS.

(b)

Balliol College MS. 149 (No. 31)
Balliol College MS. 354 (Nos. 11, 70, 80, 89)
Magdalen College MS. 60 (No. 55)
Merton College MS. 204 (No. 51)

Merton College MS. 248 (Nos. 36, 37(*b*), 38
New College MS. 88 (No. 79(*b*))
University College MS. 64 (No. 46(*a*))
University College MS. 181 (Nos. 3, 92)

III. CAMBRIDGE

(a) Cambridge University Library

Add. MS. 5943 (No. 5)
Dd. 5.64 (Nos. 19, 45)

Ee. 1.5
Ee. 1.12 (Nos. 59, 68, 90)

Ff. 2.38

Ff. 5.48 (No. 25)

Gg. 4.32 (No. 4(*b*))

Hh. 4.12 (No. 43)

Ii. 3.8

Ii. 6.2 (No. 53(*d*))

(*b*)

Fitzwilliam Museum MS. 40–1950 (No. 66)

St. John's College MS. 111

Trinity College MS. 323 (Nos. 8(*b*), 56, 84)

Trinity College MS. 1157 (Nos. 26(*b*), 89)

Trinity College MS. 1230 (No. 12)

Trinity College MS. 1450

IV. OTHER PLACES

Advocates 18.7.21 Edinburgh, National Library of Scotland (Nos. 15, 18, 22, 26(*a*), 50(*b*), 79(*a*))

Advocates 19.3.1

Bibliothèque nationale, Paris, MS. angl. 41

Bibliothèque royale, Brussels, MS. 2054.

Durham Cathedral MS. A.III, 12 (No. 20)

Ellesmere 34.B.7 Huntington Library, San Marino, Calif.

Felton MS. Victoria Public Library, Melbourne (microfilm copy in C.U.L.)

Hunterian Museum, Glasgow, MS. V.8.15 (Nos. 44, 47)

John Rylands Library, Manchester, MS. Lat. 395 (No. 24)

Trinity College, Dublin, MS. 301

Trinity College, Dublin, MS. 516

Ushaw College, Durham, MS. 10 (No. 69)

THE FALL. THE PROMISE OF REDEMPTION

1

Bodl., MS. Bodley 26, f. 200ᵛ

(a)

Adam, alas and waylaway!
A luther dede dedest thou that day!

(b)

Also Adam wyt lust and likynge
Broghte al his ken into wo and wepynge,
So schal a child of the kende springe,
That schal brynge hym and alle hyse
Into joye and blisse habbynge.   5

2

B.M., MS. Sloane 2593, f. 11ʳ

Adam lay ibowndyn, bowndyn in a bond,
Fowre thowsand wynter thowt he not to long.

And al was for an appil, an appil that he tok,
As clerkes fyndyn wretyn in here book.

Ne hadde the appil take ben, the appil take ben,   5
Ne hadde never our Lady a ben hevene qwen.

Blyssid be the tyme that appil take was,
Therfore we mown syngyn *'Deo gracias!'*

3

Heried be thou, blisful lord above,
    That vouched saaf this journé forto take,
Man to bycome, only for mannes love,
    And deth to suffren for oure synnes sake;
    So hast thou us out of the bondes shake   5
        Of Sathanas that held us longe in peyne:
        Honoured be thou, Jesu sovereyne!

Full evel I dede whan I the appul toke;
    I wende have had therby prosperite—
Hit sate so nyhe my sides that thei quoke.   10
    To grete meschief I fel fro hye degree,
    And all myn issu for bycause of me.
        Now hast thou, lord, restorid al ageyn:
        Honoured be thou, Jesu sovereyn!

So richely thou hast refresshid us,   15
    Us wel comforted with this feste ryal;
So swete a fruyt and so delicious,
    So faire it is, and so celestial,
    That oure disese now is foryeten al—
        This fruyt hath so visited every veyne.   20
        Honoured be thou, Jesu sovereyne!

This may be cleped wel the fruyt of lyf—
    The fruyt of deth was wherof I assayde,
That, by thi jugement diffinityf,
    Fyve thousand yere I was ful evill arayde,   25
    Til that this fruyt that born was of a mayde
        Had al refourmed. Lete us syng and seyn,
        Honoured be thou, Jesu soverayn!

1 Heried] *some MSS.* honured   3 to] *B.M. MS Egerton 615   MS.* man
bycome   4 oure] *other MSS.* my   10 quoke] *Eg.* ooke   14 be]
MS. bo   20 hath so visited] *Eg.   MS.* hath visited   22 cleped] *some
MSS.* called   24 thi jugement] *Eg.* thi   *MS.* this jugement   26 that
born was] *Eg.   MS.* was born   27 Lete us] *Eg.* therfor lat us seyn   *Felton
MS.* therfor lat us synge and sayn

2

ANNUNCIATION AND NATIVITY

4

(a)

B.M., MS. Harley 7322, f. 143ʳ

The yates of Parais
Thoruth Eve weren iloken;
And thoruth oure swete ladi
Ayein hui beoth nouthe open.

(b)

C.U.L., MS. Gg 4.32, f. 21ʳ

Heil, Marie, ful of wynne!
The holy gost is the withinne.
Blesced be thou over alle wymmen,
And the fruit of thin wombe! Amen.

5

C.U.L., MS. Add. 5943, f. 182ᵛ

'*Ecce, ancilla Domini!*'
  Thus seyde the virgine wythuten vyse,
Whan Gabryll grett hure gracyously:
'Hayle be thou, virgine, ipreved on prys,
  Thou shalt conceyve a swete spyce.'   5
Then seyde the virgine so myldely:
  'Therto I am ful lytel of prys,
Ecce, ancilla Domini.'

No. 5. 2, 9 wythuten] *MS.* bythute eny   *Adv. MS.* withowtyn   4–5 *Adv.*
That holy pynakell preved of price / Of the schall sprynge a full swete spice.
7 am] *Adv. MS.* han

3

'Hayle be thou, gracious, wythuten gilt,
  Mayden iboren alther best,   10
Al en thy body schal be fulfyllyt
  That profytes haveth ypreched ful prest—
  He wyl be boren of thy brest.'
Then sayde the virgine so myldely:
  'He ys to me a welcome gest,   15
Ecce, ancilla Domini.'

Then sayde that angel: 'Conseyve thou schalt
  Within thyn holy body bryght
A chyld that Jesus schal be icallyt,
  That ys gryte Godes sone of myght;   20
  Thou ert hys tabernacle idyght.'
Then seyde the virgine mildely:
  'Syth he wroght never ayeyn the ryght,
Ecce, ancilla Domini.'

'Kalle hym Jesus of Nazareth,   25
  God and man in on degre,
That on the rode schalle suffre deth,
  And regne in Davidys dignite:
  Wel goude tydynges he hath sente to the.'
Then seyde the virgine so myldely: 30
  'He schal be dyre welcome to me,
  Ecce, ancilla Domini!'

6

B.M., MS. Sloane 2593, f. 10ᵛ

  I syng of a mayden that is makeles,
  Kyng of alle kynges to here sone che ches.

9, 11 gilt, fulfyllyt] MS. gult, fulfyllyd   10 iboren] MS. ibore   12 profytes]
MS. profythes   cf. Adv. that all these prophetes han preched so preste
13 boren] MS. bore   19 icallyt] MS. icallyd   20 gryte] MS. the gryte
Adv. om. the   21 idyght] Adv.   MS. tabernacle fayre idyght   25 Naza-
reth] MS. Nazaret   27 Adv. ryght os mon schall suffer dethe   28 regne
in] Adv.   MS. regne schalle in   29 he hath] MS. hath   cf. Adv. a blestfull
worde he sende to the
  No. 6. 1 I syng of a mayden] MS. I syng A of a myden

4

He cam also stylle ther his moder was
As dew in Aprylle that fallyt on the gras.

He cam also stylle to his moderes bowr   5
As dew in Aprille that fallyt on the flour.

He cam also stylle ther his moder lay
As dew in Aprille that fallyt on the spray.

Moder and maydyn was never non but che—
Wel may swych a lady Godes moder be!   10

7

B.M., MS. Egerton 613, f. 2ʳ

Of on that is so fayr and bright
  Velud maris stella,
Brighter than the dayis light,
  Parens et puella,
Ic crie to the, thou se to me!   5
Levedy, preye thi sone for me,
  Tam pia,
That ic mote come to the,
  Maria.

Levedi, flour of alle thing,   10
  Rosa sine spina,
Thou bere Jesu, hevene king,
  Gratia divina.
Of alle thou berst the pris,
Levedi, quene of Parays   15
  Electa.
Mayde milde moder is
  Effecta.

No. 7. *Eg. had the stanzas orig. in order 1, 3, 4, 2, 5. The letters a and b beside 2 and 3 seem to imply a correction to the present order.* 1 Of on] *Trin.* for ou. 17 is] MS. es

Of kare conseil thou ert best,
  Felix fecundata;   20
Of alle wery thou ert rest,
  Mater honorata.
Bisek him wit milde mod
That for ous alle sad his blod
  In cruce,   25
That we moten comen til him
  In luce.

Al this woreld war forlore
  Eva peccatrice
Tyl our loverd was ybore   30
  De te genitrice.
With '*Ave*' it went away,
Thuster nyht, and comth the day
  Salutis;
The welle springet ut of the   35
  Virtutis.

Wel he wot he is thi sone
  Ventre quem portasti;
He wyl nout werne the thi bone,
  Parvum quem lactasti.   40
So hende and so god he is,
He havet brout ous to blis
  Superni,
That haves idut the foule pit
  Inferni.   45

8

(a)

B.M., MS. Harley 665, f. 300ᵛ

Cristus natus est:
To geff pees to men of good wyll,
To geff lyght to hem that loked ylle,
And to draw men with lowe hym tyll.

(b)

Trinity College, Cambridge, MS. 323, f. 47ᵛ

Of one stable was his halle,
His kenestol on occe stalle,
Sente Marie his burnes alle.

9

Bodl., MS. Arch. Selden B. 26, f. 14ᵛ

Nowel, nowel, nowel,
Nowel, nowel, nowel!

Owt of your slepe aryse and wake,
For God mankynd nowe hath ytake
Al of a maide without eny make;
  Of al women she bereth the belle.
    Nowel!

And thorwe a maide faire and wys
Now man is made of ful grete pris;
Now angelys knelen to mannys servys,
  And at this tyme al this byfel.
    Nowel!   10

7

Now man is brighter than the sonne;
Now man in heven an hye shal wone;
Blessyd be God this game is begonne,
   And his moder emperesse of helle.
      Nowel!   15

That ever was thralle, now ys he fre;
That ever was smalle, now grete is she;
Now shal God deme bothe the and me
   Unto his blysse yf we do wel.
      Nowel!   20

Now man may to heven wende;
Now heven and erthe to hym they bende;
He that was foo now is oure frende;
   This is no nay that y yowe telle.
      Nowel!   25

Now, blessyd brother, graunte us grace
A domesday to se thy face
And in thy courte to have a place,
   That we mow there synge nowel.
      Nowel!   30

10

Bodl., MS. Eng. poet. e. 1, f. 60ʳ

Tyrle, tyrlo,
So merylye the shepperdes began to blowe.

Abowt the fyld thei pyped full right,
Even abowt the middes off the nyght;
Adown frome heven thei saw cum a lyght.
   Tyrle, tirlo.

Off angels ther came a company   5
With mery songes and melody;
The shepperdes anonne gane them aspy.
   Tyrle, tyrlo.

'Gloria in excelsis,' the angels song,
And said how peace was present among   10
To every man that to the faith wold long.
  Tyrle, tyrlo.

The shepperdes hyed them to Bethleme
To se that blyssid sons beme,
And ther they found that glorious streme.   15
  Tyrle, tyrlo.

Now preye we to that mek chyld,
And to his mothere that is so myld,
The wich was never defylyd,
  Tyrle, tyrlo,   20

That we may cum unto his blysse
Where joy shall never mysse;
Than may we syng in paradice,
  'Tirle, tirlo.'

I pray yow all that be here   25
Fore to syng and mak good chere
In the worschip off God thys yere.
  Tyrle, tirlo.

11

Balliol College, Oxford, MS. 354, f. 224^r

     Can I not syng but hoy,
     Whan the joly sheperd made so mych joy.

     The sheperd upon a hill he satt;
     He had on hym his tabard and his hat,

No. 10. 10 how] *MS.* who

9

Hys tarbox, hys pype, and hys flagat;
Hys name was called Joly, Joly Wat,
   For he was a gud herdes boy.   5
      With hoy!
   For in hys pype he made so mych joy.

The sheperd upon a hill was layd;
Hys doge to hys gyrdyll was tayd;
He had not slept but a lytill brayd   10
But 'Gloria in excelcis' was to hym sayd.
      With hoy!
   For in his pipe he mad so myche joy.

The sheperd on a hill he stode;
Rownd abowt hym his shepe they yode;   15
He put hys hond under hys hode;
He saw a star as rede as blod.
      With hoy!
   For in his pipe he mad so myche joy.

'Now farwell Mall, and also Will;   20
For my love go ye all styll
Unto I cum agayn you till,
And evermore, Will, ryng well thy bell.'
      With hoy!
   For in his pipe he mad so mych joy.   25

'Now must I go ther Cryst was borne;
Farewell, I cum agayn tomorn;
Dog, kepe well my shep fro the corn,
And warn well Warroke when I blow my horn.'
      With hoy!   30
   For in hys pype he made so mych joy.

The sheperd sayd anonryght,
'I will go se yon farly syght,

6, 12 etc. With] *MS.* V*ith*   10 brayd] *MS.* broyd

10

Wheras the angell syngith on hight,
And the star that shynyth so bryght.'   35
   With hoy!
  For in [his] pipe he made so mych joy.

Whan Wat to Bedleem cum was,
He swet—he had gon faster than a pace.
He fownd Jesu in a sympyll place   40
Betwen an ox and an asse.
   With hoy!
  For in his pipe he mad so mych joy.

'Jesu, I offer to the here my pype,
My skyrte, my tarbox, and my scrype;   45
Home to my fellowes now will I skype,
And also loke unto my shepe.'
   With hoy!
  For in his pipe he mad so myche joy.

'Now, farewell, myne own herdesman Wat.'   50
'Ye, for God, lady, even so I hat.
Lull well Jesu in thy lape,
And farewell, Joseph, wyth thy rownd cape.'
   With hoy!
  For in hys pipe he mad so myche joy.   55

'Now may I well both hope and syng,
For I have bene a Crystes beryng.
Home to my felowes now wyll I flyng.
Cryst of hevyn to his blis us bryng!'
   With hoy!   60
  For in his pipe he mad so myche joy.

38 Bedleem] MS. Bedlem   45 MS. transposes skyrte and scrype.

Trinity College, Cambridge, MS. 1230

Ther is no rose of swych vertu
As is the rose that bare Jesu.

Ther is no rose of swych vertu
As is the rose that bar Jesu;
Allelyua.

For in this rose conteynyd was
Heven and erthe in lytyl space,   5
Res miranda.

Be that rose we may weel see
That he is God in personys thre,
Pari forma.

The aungelys sungyn the sheperdes to: 10
'Gloria in excelcis Deo.'
Gaudeamus.

Leve we al this wordly merthe,
And folwe we this joyful berthe;
Transeamus.   15

13

B.M., MS. Sloane 2593, f. 32ʳ

'Lullay, myn lykyng, my dere sone, myn swetyng,
Lullay, my dere herte, myn owyn dere derlyng.'

I saw a fayr maydyn syttyn and synge;
Sche lullyd a lytyl chyld, a swete lordyng.

That eche Lord is that that made alle thinge;
Of alle lordis he is Lord, of alle kynges Kyng.

Ther was mekyl melody at that chyldes berthe;   5
Alle tho wern in hevene blys, thei made mekyl merthe.

Aungele bryght, thei song that nyght and seydyn to that chyld,
'Blyssid be thou, and so be sche that is bothe mek and myld.'

Prey we now to that chyld, and to his moder dere,
Grawnt hem his blyssyng that now makyn chere.   10

14

B.M., MS. Harley 7322, f. 135ᵛ

Jesu, swete sone dere,
On porful bed list thou here,
    And that me greveth sore;
For thi cradel is ase a bere,
Oxe and asse beth thi fere—   5
    Weepe ich mai tharfore.

Jesu, swete, beo not wroth
Thou ich nabbe clout ne cloth
    The on for to folde,
The on to folde ne to wrappe,   10
For ich nabbe clout ne lappe—
Bote ley thou thi fet to my pappe
    And wite the from the colde.

15

N.L.S., MS. Advocates 18.7.21, f. 6ʳ

Lullay, lullay, litel child,
    Qui wepest thou so sore?

Lullay, lullay, litel child,
Thou that were so sterne and wild
Nou art become meke and mild
    To saven that was forlore.

No. 14. 7 not] MS. noth

But for my senne I wot it is   5
That Godis sone suffret this;
Merci, Lord! I have do mis;
    Iwis, I wile no more.

Ayenis my Fadris wille I ches
An appel with a reuful res;   10
Werfore myn hertage I les,
    And nou thou wepist therfore.

An appel I tok of a tre;
God it hadde forboden me;
Werfore I sulde dampned be,   15
    Yef thi weping ne wore.

Lullay, for wo, thou litel thing,
Thou litel barun, thou litel king;
Mankindde is cause of thi murning,
    That thou hast loved so yore.   20

For man, that thou hast ay loved so,
Yet saltu suffren peines mo,
In heved, in feet, in hondis to,
    And yet wepen wel more.

That peine us make of senne fre;   25
That peine us bringge, Jesu, to the;
That peine us helpe ay to fle
    The wikkede fendes lore.

16

Lully, lulla, thow littell tine child,
By, by, lully, lullay, thow littell tyne child,
    By, by, lully, lullay.

14

O sisters too,
How may we do
  For to preserve this day
This pore yongling
For whom we do singe,   5
  'By, by, lully, lullay'?

Herod the king
In his raging,
  Chargid he hath this day
His men of might   10
In his owne sight
  All yonge children to slay.

That wo is me,
Pore child, for thee,
  And ever morne and may   15
For thi parting
Nether say nor singe,
  'By, by, lully, lullay.'

THE PASSION OF CHRIST

17

Bodl., MS. Bodley 791, f. 64^r

Ellas! mornyngh y syngh, mornyng y cal;
Our lord ys deyd that boghte ous al.

No. 17. 2 boghte] *MS.* bogthe

N.L.S., MS. Advocates 18.7.21, f. 119ᵛ

A sory beverech it is and sore it is abouht
Nou in this sarpe time this brewing hat me brouht.
Fader, if it mowe ben don als I have besouht,
Do awey this beverich, that I ne drink et nouht.

And if it mowe no betre ben, for alle mannis gilt,   5
That it ne muste nede that my blod be spilt,
Suete fader, I am thi sone, thi wil be fulfilt,
I am her thin owen child, I wil don as thou wilt.

19

C.U.L., MS. Dd. 5.64, III, f. 34ᵛ

My trewest tresowre sa trayturly was taken,
Sa bytterly bondyn wyth bytand bandes—
How sone of thi servandes was thou forsaken,
And lathly for my lufe hurld with thair handes!

My well of my wele sa wrangwysly wryed,   5
So pulled owt of preson to Pylate at prime:
Thaire dulles and thaire dyntes ful drerely thou dreed
When thai schot in thi syght bath slaver and slyme.

My hope of my hele sa hyed to be hanged,
Sa charged with thi crosce and corond with thorne,   10
Ful sare to thi hert thi steppes tha stanged;
Me thynk thi bak burd breke—it bendes forborne!

My salve of my sare sa saryful in syght,
Sa naked and nayled thi ryg on the rode,
Ful hydusly hyngand, thay heved the on hyght,   15
Thai lete the stab in the stane all stekked that thar stode.

No. 18. *MS.* abouth, brouth, besouth, nouth; gilth, spilth.

My dereworthly derlyng, sa dolefully dyght,
Sa straytly upryght streyned on the rode;
For thi mykel mekenes, thi mercy, thi myght,
Thow bete al my bales with bote of thi blode.   20

My fender of my fose, sa fonden in the felde,
Sa lufly lyghtand at the evensang tyde;
Thi moder and hir menyhe unlaced thi scheld—
All weped that thar were, thi woundes was sa wyde.

My pereles prynce als pure I the pray,   25
The mynde of this myrour thou lat me noght mysse;
Bot wynd up my wylle to won wyth the ay,
That thou be beryd in my brest, and bryng me to blysse.

20

Durham Cathedral, MS. A.III. 12, f. 49^r

Whyt was hys nakede brest and red of blode hys syde,
Bleyc was his fair andled, his wnde dop ant wide,
And hys armes ystreit hey upon the rode;
On fif studes on his body the stremes ran o blode.

21

Bodl. MS. Arch. Selden, supra 74, f. 55^v

Nou goth sonne under wod,
Me reweth, Marie, thi faire rode.
Nou goth sonne under tre,
Me reweth, Marie, thi sone and the.

No. 20. 1 Whyt] MS. wyth   3 ystreit] MS. ystreith

17

22

N.L.S., MS. Advocates 18.7.21, f. 24ʳ

Wy have ye no reuthe on my child?
　　Have reuthe on me ful of murning!
Taket doun on rode my derworthi child,
　　Or prek me on rode with my derling!

More pine ne may me ben don　　　　　　　　5
　　Than laten me liven in sorwe and schame—
Als love me bindet to my sone,
　　So lat us deyyen bothen isame!

23

B.M., MS. Royal 12. E. 1, f. 193ʳ

'Stond wel, moder, under rode,
　　Biheld thi child wyth glade mode;
　　　　Blythe moder mictu be.'
'Sune, hu may I blithe stonden?
I se thin feet, I se thin honden　　　　　　　5
　　　　Nayled to the harde tre.'

'Moder, do wey thi wepinge;
I thole this ded for mannes thinge—
　　　　For owen gilte tholi non.'
'Sune, I fele the dede-stunde;　　　　　　　10
The swerd is at min herte-grunde
　　　　That me byhycte Symeon.'

No. 23. 3 be] *MS.* ben　　　4 *MS.* sune quu may blithe stonden

'Moder, reu upon thi beren!
Thou wasse awey tho blodi teren;
   It doth me werse than mi ded.'   15
'Sune, hu micti teres wernen?
I se tho blodi flodes ernen
   Ut of thin herte to min fet.'

'Moder, nu y may the seye,
Bettere is that ic one deye   20
   Than al mankyn to helle go.'
'Sune, y se thi bodi swngen,
Thi brest, thin hond, thi fot thurstungen;
   No selli nis thou me be wo.'

'Moder, if y dar the telle,   25
Yif y ne deye thou gost to helle;
   I thole this ded for thine sake.'
'Sune, thou best me so minde,
Ne wit me nout—it is mi kinde
   That y for the this sorwe make.'   30

'Moder, merci! let me deyen
For Adam ut of helle beyen,
   And al mankin that is forloren.'
'Sune, wat sal me to rede?
Thi pine pineth me to dede;   35
   Let me deyn the biforen.'

'Moder, nutarst thou miht leren
Wat pine tholen that childre beren,
   What sorwe haven that child forgon.'
'Sune y wot, y kan the telle—   40
Bute it be the pine of helle
   More sorwe ne wot y non.'

13 beren] *MS.* bern   15 doth] *MS.* don   19 seye] *MS.* seyn   24 nis]
Bodl. Ms. Digby 86   MS. om.   25 telle] *MS.* tellen   29 Ne wit me]
MS. with me   *cf. MS. Harley 2253* Ne wyt me   30 this sorwe] *H.   MS.* Sorye
32 beyen] *MS.* beyn   35 pineth] *MS* pined   *H.* pyneth   37 miht] *MS.*
mith   40 telle] *MS.* tellen   42 wot] *MS.* woth

'Moder, reu of moder kare!
Nu thou wost of moder fare,
   Thou thou be clene mayden-man.'   45
'Sune, help at alle nede,
Alle tho that to me grede,
   Mayden, wyf, and fol wymman.'

'Moder, y may no lengore duelle,
The time is cumen y fare to helle,   50
   The thridde day y rise upon.'
'Sune, y wyle with the funde,
y deye, ywis, of thine wnde,
   So reuful ded was nevere non.'

When he ros than fel thi sorwe,   55
The blisse sprong the thridde morwe—
   Blithe moder wer thou tho.
Moder for that ilke blisse
Bisech ure god ure sinnes lisse,
   Thou be ure cheld ayen ure fo.   60

Blisced be thou, quen of hevene,
Bring us ut of helle levene
   Thurh thi dere sunes miht.
Loverd, for that ilke blode
That thou sadde upon the rode,   65
   Led us into hevene liht.

46 at alle nede] *H.*   *MS.* alle at nede   47 grede] *MS.* greden   49 ff. *A corner of the page of the MS. is lost.*   49 lengore] *from H.*   duelle] *MS.* duellen 51 thridde day] *from H.*   52 with the] *H.*   *MS.* withe   53 deye ywis] *from H.* wnde] *MS.* wnden   55 When] *from H. Corner of MS. torn off.*   56 *completed from H.*   57 Blithe moder] *H.*   *MS.* wen blithe   58 *completed from H.* 59 lisse] *MS.* lesse   60 cheld] *MS.* chel   63 Thurh] *MS.* thurth   63, 66 *MS.* mith,lith   64 *from H.*   *MS.* Moder for that hithe blode   65 thou] *MS.* that he sadde] *H.* sheddest   *MS. Trin. Coll. Dublin 301* bledes

24

  Sodenly afraide, half wakyng, half slepyng,
  And gretly dismayde—a wooman sate weepyng,

With favoure in hir face ferr passyng my reason,
And of hir sore weepyng this was the enchesone:
Hir soon in hir lap lay, she seid, slayne by treason.   5
Yif wepyng myght ripe bee, it seemyd than in season.
      'Jesu!' so she sobbid—
      So hir soon was bobbid,
      And of his lif robbid—
  Saying thies wordes, as I say thee: 10
  'Who cannot wepe, come lerne at me.'

I said I cowd not wepe, I was so harde hartid.
Shee answerd me shortly with wordys that smarted:
'Lo, nature shall move the; thou must be converted;
Thyne owne Fader this nyght is deed'—lo, thus she thwarted— 15
      'So my soon is bobbid,
      And of his lif robbid.'
      Forsooth than I sobbid,
  Veryfyng the wordes she seid to me:
  'Who cannot wepe may lern at me.'   20

'Now breke, hert, I the pray! this cors lith so rulye,
So betyn, so wowndid, entreted so Jewlye.
What wight may me behold and wepe nat? Noon truly,
To see my deed dere soon lygh bleedyng, lo, this newlye.'
      Ever stil she sobbid—   25
      So hir soon was bobbid,
      And of his lif robbid—
  Newyng the wordes, as I say thee:
  'Who cannot wepe, com lern at me.'

13 shortly . . . wordys] *T.* *MS.* with wordys shortly   20 me] *MS.* the

On me she caste hir ey, said, 'See, man, thy brothir!' 30
She kissid hym and said, 'Swete, am I not thy modir?'
In sownyng she fill there—it wolde be noon othir;
I not which more deedly, the toon or the tothir.
>> Yit she revived and sobbid,
>> So hir soon was bobbid, 35
>> And of his lif robbid—
'Who cannot wepe,' this was the laye,
And with that word she vanysht away.

25

C.U.L., MS. Ff. 5.48, f. 73^r

O alle women that ever were borne
>> That berys childur, abyde and se
How my son liggus me beforne
>> Upon my skyrte, takyn fro tre.
>> Your childur ye dawnse upon your kne 5
With laghyng, kyssyng, and mery chere;
>> Beholde my childe, beholde now me,
For now liggus ded my dere son dere.

O woman, woman, wel is the!
>> Thy childis cap thou dose upon; 10
Thou pykys his here, beholdys his ble,
>> Thou wost not wele when thou hast done.
>> But ever, alas! I make my mone
To se my sonnys hed as hit is here;
>> I pyke owt thornys be on and on, 15
For now liggus ded my dere son dere.

O woman, a chaplet chosyn thou has
>> Thy childe to were, hit dose the gret likyng—

No. 25. 1 O] *MSS.* off 4 skyrte] *C.U.L. MS. Ff. 2.38.* *MS* kne 7 now]
Ff. 2.38 wele 18 *Ff. 2.38* dose the likyng

Thou pynnes hit on with gret solas!
  And I sitte with my son sore wepyng,   20
  His chaplet is thornys sore prickyng,
His mouth I kys with a carfull chere—
  I sitte wepyng and thou syngyng,
For now liggus ded my dere son dere.

O woman, loke to me agayne,   25
  That playes and kisses your childur pappys.
To se my son I have gret payne,
  In his brest so gret a gap is
  And on his body so mony swappys.
With blody lippys I kis hym here,   30
  Alas! full hard me thynk me happys,
For now liggus ded my dere son dere.

O woman, thou takis thi childe be the hand
  And seis, 'My son, gif me a strake!'
My sonnys handis ar sore bledand;   35
  To loke on hym me list not layke.
  His handis he suffyrd for thi sake
Thus to be boryd with nayles sere;
  When thou makes myrth gret sorow I make,
For now liggus ded my dere son, dere.   40

Beholde women, when that ye play
  And hase your childur on knees daunsand,
Ye fele ther fete, so fete ar thay,
  And to your sight ful wel likand.
  But the most fyngur of myn hande   45
Thorow my sonnys fete I may put here
  And pulle hit out sore bledand,
For now liggus ded my dere son dere.

---

19 *Ff. 2.38* grete joye thou mas   28 a] *Ff. 2.38* *MS. om.*   34 strake]
MS. stroke   38 nayles sere] *Ff. 2.38* *MS.* nayle and speyre   43 *Ff. 2.38*
MS. he fele therfor fittys or day   45 myn] *Ff. 2.38* *MS.* any

Therfor, women, be town and strete
   Your childur handis when ye beholde,   50
Theyr brest, theire body, and theire fete,
   Then gode hit were on my son thynk ye wolde,
   How care has made my hert ful colde
To se my son, with nayle and speyre,
   With scourge and thornys manyfolde,   55
Woundit and ded, my dere son dere.

Thou hase thi son full holl and sounde,
   And myn is ded upon my kne;
Thy childe is lawse and myn is bounde,
   Thy childe is an life, and myn ded is he—   60
   Whi was this oght but for the?
For my childe trespast never here.
   Me thynk ye be holdyne to wepe with me,
For now liggus ded my dere son dere.

Wepe with me, both man and wyfe,   65
   My childe is youres and lovys yow wele.
If your childe had lost his life
   Ye wolde wepe at every mele;
   But for my son wepe ye never a del.
If ye luf youres, myne has no pere;   70
   He sendis youris both hap and hele,
And for yow dyed my dere son dere.

Now, alle wymmen that has your wytte,
   And sees my childe on my knees ded,
Wepe not for yours but wepe for hit,   75
   And ye shall have full mycull mede.
   He wolde agayne for your luf blede
Rather or that ye damned were.
   I pray yow all to hym take hede,
For now liggus ded my dere son dere.   80

Farewel, woman, I may no more
    For drede of deth reherse his payne.
Ye may lagh when ye list and I wepe sore,
    That may ye se and ye loke to me agayne.
    To luf my son and ye be fayne   85
I wille luff yours with hert entere,
    And he shall brynge your chyldur and yow sertayne
To blisse wher is my dere son dere.

COMPLAINTS OF CHRIST

26

N.L.S., MS. Advocates 18.7.21, f. 125^v

(a)

Ye that pasen be the weyye,
    Abidet a litel stounde:
Beholdet, al mi felawes,
    Yef ani me lik is founde.
To the tre with nailes thre   5
    Wol fast I hange bounde;
With a spere al thoru mi side
    To min herte is made a wounde.

(b)

Trinity College, Cambridge, MS. 1157, f. 69^r

O man unkynde,
Have thow yn mynde
    My passyon smert,
Thou shall me fynde
To the full kynde—   5
    Lo, here my hert!

B.M., MS. Harley 4012, f. 109^r

> Wofully araide,
>   My blode, man,
>   For the ran,
> Hit may not be naide,
>   My body blo and wanne,   5
> Wofully araide.

Beholde me, I pray the, with all thyne hole reson,
And be not hard hertid, for this encheson:
That I for thi saule sake was slayne, in good seson,
Begilid and betraide by Judas fals treson,   10
    Unkindly intretid,
    With sharp corde sore fretid,
    The Jues me thretid,
  They mowid, they spittid, and disspisid me,
  Condemned to deth as thou maiste se.   15

Thus nakid am I nailid, O man, for thi sake.
I love the, thenne love me. Why slepist thou? awake!
Remember my tender hert-rote for the brake,
With paynes my vaines constrayned to crake.
    Thus was I defasid,   20
    Thus was my flesh rasid,
    And I to deth chasid,
  Like a lambe led unto sacrefise,
  Slayne I was in most cruell wise.

Of sharp thorne I have worne a crowne on my hed,   25
So rubbid, so bobbid, so rufulle, so red,
Sore payned, sore strayned, and for thi love ded,
Unfayned, not demed, my blod for the shed,

14 they] *MS*. the   *Fayrfax MS*. they grynned, they scornyd me   20 Thus]
MS. this   *F*. Thus toggid to and fro / Thus wrappid all in woo, / Whereas never
man was so / Entretid, thus in most cruell wise / Was like a lombe offerd in
sacrifice.   26–7 *F*. So paynyd, so straynyd, so rufull, so red / Thus bobbid,
thus robbid, thus for thi love ded.   28 demed] *F*. deynyd   *'Heber' copy*
(*Dyce*) drynyde

My fete and handis sore,
With sturde naylis bore;   30
What myght I suffer more
Then I have sufferde, man, for the?
Com when thou wilt, and welcome to me.

Dere brother, non other thing I desire,
But geve me thi hert fre, to rewarde myne hire.   35
I am he that made the erth, water, and fire.
Sathanas, that sloven and right lothely sire,
        Hym have I overcaste,
        In hell presoune bounde faste,
        Wher ay his woo shall laste.   40
I have purvaide a place full clere
For mankynde, whom I have bought dere.

28

B.M., MS. Harley 2316, f. 25ʳ

Men rent me on rode
With wndes woliche wode;
Al blet mi blode—
Thenk, man, al it is the to gode!

Thenk who the first wroghte,   5
For what werk helle thow sowhte,
Thenk who the ageyn bowhte—
Werk warli, fayle me nowhte.

Biheld mi side,
Mi wndes sprede so wide;   10
Restles I ride.
Lok upon me! Put fro the pride.

No. 27. 30 With] F. the   32 sufferde, man] F. done, O man   33 wilt, and
welcome] F. lyst, wellcum   34 ff. This stanza not in F.   36–42 H. y
wrought the, I bowght the frome eternal fyre / y pray the aray the tooward my
hyght empyre / [ab]ove the oryent / wheroff y am regent / lord god omny-
potent / wyth me too reyn yn endlys welthe / remember man thy sawlys helthe.
No. 28. 2 With] MS. wiht (so ll. 14, 23)   4 the] MS. ʒe (so throughout)

Mi palefrey is of tre,
With nayles naylede thwrh me.
Ne is more sorwe to se—   15
Certes noon more no may be!

Under mi gore
Ben wndes selcowthe sore.
Ler, man, mi lore—
For mi love sinne no more.   20

Fal nowht for fonding,
That schal the most turne to goode;
Mak stif withstonding—
Thenk wel who me rente on the rode.

29

B.M., MS. Add. 46919, f. 206^r

My volk, what habbe y do the,
Other in what thyng toened the?
Gyn nouthe and onswere thou me.

Vor vrom Egypte ich ladde the,
Thou me ledest to rode tre.   5
    My volk, what habbe y do the,
    Other in what thyng toened the?
    Gyn nouthe and onswere thou me.

Thorou wyldernesse ich ladde the,
And vourty yer bihedde the,   10
And aungeles bred ich yaf to the,
And into reste ich brouhte the.
    My volk etc.

No. 28. 19 Ler] MS. der
No. 29. 5 tre] MS. troe (so l. 34)

What more shulde ich haven ydon
That thou ne havest nouht undervon?
   My volk etc.

Ich the vedde, and shrudde the;   15
And thou wyth eysyl drinkest to me,
And wyth spere styngest me.
   My volk etc.

Ich Egypte boet vor the,
And hoere tem y shlou vor the.
   My volk etc.

I delede the see vor the,   20
And Pharaon dreynte vor the;
And thou to princes sullest me.
   My volk etc.

In bem of cloude ich ladde the;
And to Pylate thou ledest me.
   My volk etc.

Wyth aungeles mete ich vedde the;   25
And thou bufetest and scourgest me.
   My volk etc.

Of the ston ich dronk to thee;
And thou wyth galle drincst to me.
   My volk etc.

Kynges of Chanaan ich vor the bet;
And thou betest myn heved wyth red.   30
   My volk etc.

Ich yaf the croune of kynedom;
And thou me yyfst a croune of thorn.
   My volk etc.

14 nouht] *MS.* nouth   15 vedde] *MS.* vedde wel *with* wel *deleted*
18 boet] *MS.* boeth   22 sullest] *the scribe has deleted* soldest   24 ledest]
MS. corrected from laddest   29 bet] *MS.* boet   30 betest] *MS.* boete
corrected to betest   red] *MS.* roed   32 yyfst] *MS.* ȝeve *corrected to* yyfst

Ich muchel worshype doede to the;
And thou me hongest on rode tre.
My volk etc.

30

Bodl., MS. Bodley 416, f. 106ʳ

Jesus doth him bymene,
   And speketh to synful mon:
'Thi garland is of grene,
   Of floures many on;
Myn of sharpe thornes,   5
   Myn hewe it maketh won.

'Thyn hondes streite gloved,
   White and clene kept;
Myne with nailes thorled
   On rode, and eke my feet.   10

'Acros thou berest thyn armes,
   Whan thou dauncest narewe;
To me hastou non awe,
But to worldes glorie—
   Myne for the on rode   15
   With the Jewes wode
With grete ropis todraw.

'Opyne thou hast thi syde—
Spaiers longe and wide—
For veyn glorie and pride,   20
And thi longe knyf astrout—
Thou ert of the gai route:
Myn with spere sharpe
   Ystongen to the herte;
   My body with scourges smerte   25
Biswongen al aboute.

No. 29. 34 hongest] *MS.* henge, *corrected to* hongest   tre] *MS.* troe

'Al that y tholede on rode for the,
   To me was shame and sorwe;
Wel litel thou lovest me,
And lasse thou thenkest on me,   30
   An evene and eke amorwe.

'Swete brother, wel myght thou se
Thes peynes stronge in rode tre
Have y tholed for love of the;
Thei that have wrought it me   35
   May synge welawo.
Be thou kynde pur charite,
Let thi synne and love thou me,
Hevene blisse y shal yeve the,
   That lasteth ay and oo.'   40

THE MEMORY OF CHRIST'S PASSION

31

Balliol College, Oxford, MS. 149, f. 31ᵛ

The mynde of thy swet passion, Jesu—
   Teres it tolles,
   Eyene it bolles,
   My vesage it wetes,
   And my hert it swetes.   5

32

Bodl., MS. Digby 2, f. 6ʳ

I sike, al wan I singe,
   For sorue that I se
Wan ic wit wepinge
   Biholde apon the tre:

No. 31. 2 tolles] *MS*. telles   3 Eyene] *corrected from* ene

I se Jesu, mi suete, 5
  His herte blode forlete
For the luve of me.
  His wondis waxin wete—
  Marie, milde and suete
Thou haf merci of me! 10

Hey apon a dune
  As al folke hit se may,
A mile wythute the tune
  Abute the mid-day,
    The rode was op areride 15
    His frendis werin afered—
  Thei clungin so the cley—
    The rod stont in ston;
    Mari hirselfe alon—
  Hir songe was 'wayleway!' 20

Wan ic him biholde
  Wyt ey and herte bo
I se his bodi colde,
  His ble waxit alle bloe.
    He hongeth al of blode 25
    Se hey apon the rode
  Bitwixin thefis two—
    Hu soldi singe mor?
    Mari, thou wepe sor,
  Thou wist of al his woe. 30

Wel ofte wan I sike,
  I make mi mone;
Ivel hit may me like—
  Ande wondir nis hit non—

9 suete] *MS.* (?) sute   15 was] *MS. Harl. 2253* is   16 werin] *MS.*
werin al   *H.* aren   17 clungin] *H.* clyngeth   18 stont] *MS.* stonit
20 was wayleway] *MS.* was wayl. . . . (*the edge of the page is now very faded*)
H. seith weylaway   22 bo] *H.*   *MS.* bothe   25 hongeth] *MS.* honge
    thou] *MS.* thw   31 sike] *MS.* Siche

Wan I se honge hey,   35
  Ande bitter peynis drei
Jesu mi lemmon;
  His wondis sor smerte,
  The sper is at his herte
And thorh his side gon.   40

The naylis beit al to stronge,
  The smyth is al to sleye;
Thou bledis al to longe,
  The tre is al to heye.
  The stonis waxin wete—   45
  Allas! Jesu mi suete,
Feu frendis hafdis neye,
  But sin Jon murnind
  And Mari wepind,
That al thi sorue seye.   50

Wel ofte wan I slepe
  With soru ic am thourhsoht,
Wan I wake and wepe
  I thenke in mi thoht:
  Allas! that men beit wode,   55
  Biholdit an the rode
And silit (ic li noht)
  Her souelis into sin
  For any worldis win,
That was so der iboght.   60

33

B.M., MS. Royal 12. E. 1, f. 194ᵛ

Quanne ic se on rode
  Jesu mi lemman,
An besiden him stonden
  Marie an Johan,

No. 32. 40 thorh . . . gon] *MS.* thorit . . . gun   41 stronge] *H.*   *MS.* longe
52 thourhsoht (54 thoht, 57 noht 60 iboght)] *MS.* thoit soit (thoit, noyt, hiboyt)
H. thourhsoht   53 wepe] *MS.* wende.   59 worldis] *MS.* worldehis

And his rig iswungen,   5
And his side istungen,
   For the luve of man
Wel ou ic to wepen
And sinnes forleten,
   Yif ic of luve kan,   10
   Yif ic of luve kan,
   Yif ic of luve kan.

34

Bodl., MS. Douce 295, f. 143ʳ

Whan I thinke on Cristes blod
That he schad upon the rode,
   I lete teris smerte.
What man may be onkende
That Cristis blod hath in mende   5
   And enterly in his herte.

Swete Jesu Crist what is thine gilte
That thus for me thou arte spilte,
   Floure of unlothfulnesse?
I am a thef and thou deyiste,   10
I am gilti and thou abeyist
   Al myn wickidnesse.

Whi yave thou so mekil for thine,
What wenyst thou with thine harde pine,
   Riche in blisse above?   15
Love thine herte so depe hath soughte
That peyne of deth lettith the nought
   To winne manys love.

No. 33. 5 iswungen] *MS.* isuongen
No. 34. 14 pine] *MS.* peyne   15 above] *MS.* abovyn

35

B.M. MS. Arundel 286, f. 3ʳ

Jesus woundes so wide
  Ben welles of lif to the goode,
Namely the stronde of hys syde,
  That ran ful breme on the rode.

Yif thee liste to drinke,   5
  To flee fro the fendes of helle,
Bowe thou doun to the brinke
  And mekely taste of the welle.

36

Merton College, Oxford, MS. 248, f. 167ʳ

Steddefast crosse, inmong alle other
Thow art a tre mykel of prise,
In brawnche and flore swylk another
  I ne wot non in wode ne rys.
Swete be the nalys, and swete be the tre,   5
And sweter be the birdyn that hangis uppon the!

THE TRIUMPH OF CHRIST

37

(a)

B.M., MS. Add. 46919, f. 210ᵛ

He sthey opon the rode, that barst helle clos;
Ygurd he was wyth strengthe ,the thrydde day aros.

(b)

Merton College, Oxford, MS. 248, f. 139ᵛ

I sayh hym with fless al bisprad: he cam vram Est.
I sayh hym with blod al byssad: he cam vram West.
I sayh thet manye he with hym broughte: he cam vram South.
I sayh thet the world of hym ne roughte: he cam vram North.

'I come vram the wedlok as a suete spouse thet habbe my wif
    with me innome. 5
I come vram vight a staleworthe knyght, thet myne vo habbe
    overcome.
I come vram the chepyng as a riche chapman, thet mankynde
    habbe ibought.
I come vram an uncouthe londe as a sely pylegrym, thet ferr
    habbe isought.'

38

Merton College, Oxford, MS. 248, f. 141ᵛ

    An ernemorwe the daylight spryngeth,
    The angles in hevene murye syngeth,
    The world is blithe and ek glad,
    The vendus of helle beth sorwuel and mad.

    Whanne the kyng, Godus sone, 5
    The strengthe of the deth hadde overcome;
    Helle dore he brake with his fot,
    And out of pyne us wreches he tok.

39

B.M., MS. Arundel 285, f. 174ᵛ

    O mothir of God, inviolat Virgin Mary,
      Exult in joy and consolacioun!
    On loft is ryssyn the gret illumynary,
      The lampe that lichtnes every regioun.

No. 37 (b) 5 habbe] *MS.* habbbe   6 *MS.* vo *written above* enemy
No. 38. 1 the] *MS.* de
No. 39. 3 illumynary] *MS.* illumynar

Thy glorius birth, the blisfull orient soune,   5
    With joy is partit fra the subtell nycht;
His bemes persit hes the skyis doun,
    Quhois blyssit uprissing glades every wycht.

Be glaid, ye angellis and ye archangellis cleir!
    Youre wailyeand prince, victorius in battale,   10
Met with all hevinlie melody and cheir;
    And to youre king ye sing, 'Haill, victour, haill!'
    That hes in erd ourecumyn with gret travale,
    And hes of hell the power put to flicht,
And thair strang portes privilie done assale,   15
    Quhois glaid uprissing blithis every wicht.

Be blicht, mankind, and gif God laude and glore,
    That hes thi lyne relaxit of the Lymbe
Quhilk. . . . .
    . . . into presoun sumtyme dirk and dym,   20
    Honour with houres and with antane and hyme
        The saikles lorde, that slane was for thi slycht,
    The pasche lambe, that on the croce did clym,
        Quhois blith uprissing glaides every wycht.

The mychty, strange, victorius campyoun,   25
    With hie imperiall laude hes done returne,
With palme of glory and with lawre croune,
    With his allweilding father to sojurne
Quhois palice hie schynes abone Saturn,
    Off quhame etheriall sternes takis licht,   30
Quhome hevin and erd dois honour and adurn,
    Quhois glaid uprissing blithis every wycht.

Wnto his trone, with hie tryumphald tryne,
    Is gone this glorius prince of most degre,
With sang of all the angellis ordouris nyne,   35
    Off sound excellyng in suavite—

5 soune] MS. sone   10 battale] MS. battall   13 travale] MS. travell
19–20 MS. quhilk into presoun   28 sojurne] MS. sojorne

To quhois incomprehensable majeste,
    Superlatyve and innosable mycht,
Be infynite laude in tyme and unite,
    Quhois glaid uprissing blithis every wycht.   40

40

B.M., MS. Add. 46919, f. 210ʳ

'What ys he, thys lordling, that cometh vrom the vyht
Wyth blod-rede wede so grysliche ydyht,
So vayre ycoyntised, so semlich in syht,
So styflyche yongeth, so douhti a knyht?'
'Ich hyt am, ich hyt am, that ne speke bote ryht,   5
Chaunpyon to helen monkunde in vyht.'

'Why thoenne ys thy shroud red wyth blod al ymeind,
As troddares in wrynge wyth most al byspreynd?'

'The wrynge ich habbe ytrodded al mysulf on,
And of al monkunde ne was non other won.   10
Ich hoem habbe ytrodded in wrethe and in grome,
And al my wede ys byspreynd with hoere blod ysome,
And al my robe yvuled to hoere grete shome.
The day of thylke wreche leveth in my thouht,
The yer of medes yeldyng ne voryet ich nouht.   15
Ich loked al aboute som helpynge mon,
Ich souhte al the route, bote help nas ther non.
Hyt was myn oune strengthe that thys bote wrouhte,
Myn owe douhtynesse that help ther me brouhte.
Ich habbe ytrodded the volk in wrethe and in grome,   20
Adreynt al wyth shennesse, ydrawe doun wyth shome.'

On Godes mylsfolnesse ich wole bythenche me,
And heryen hym in alle thyng that he yeldeth me.

No. 40. 5 *MS* ne *inserted above the line*

CHRIST'S LOVE FOR SINFUL MAN

41

Lambeth Palace, MS. 557, f. 185ᵛ.

Allas! allas! wel yvel y sped!
For synne Jesu fro me ys fled,
  That lyvely fere.
At my dore he standes al one,
And kallys 'Undo!' with reuful mone,   5
  On this manere:

'Undo, my lef, my dowve dere!
Undo! Wy stond y stekyn out here?
  Ik am thi make!
Lo, my heved and myne lockys   10
Ar al bywevyd wyth blody dropys
  For thine sake.'

42

Victoria and Albert Museum, MS. Dyce 45, f. 21ᵛ

Swete harte be trwe!
Chaunge for no newe,
  Come home to me agene!
I shall full swetely
Take the to mercye,   5
  And delyver the owte of payne.

When thou arte synfull
My harte ys paynefull
  And bledynge for thy sake:
Yete onece remember   10
Howe my harte tender
  Will the to mercy take.

No. 41. 1 wel] *MS.* vel   5 with] *MS.* yit   8 y] *MS. omits*   9 Ik] *MS.*
Iyk   11 wyth] *MS.* wyt
No. 42. 2 *MS.* chavnge for newe

39

Then, love, be trwe,
Come and renewe
   Thyselfe yet wonse agayne— 15
I shall full swetely
Take the to mercye,
   And delyver the owte of payne.

A wounde full wyde,
Deape in my syde 20
   Was pearsed for thi sake,
To grawnte the grace
For thy trespace—
   Thou mayste thi sorow slake.

My dear harte trwe, 25
Come and renewe
   Thyselfe yete onse agayne:
Some tyme remember
Howe my harte tender
   Thus for thi sake was slayne. 30

Thys lover trwe,
Whoo wolde renewe
   Mans soule to vertuouse lyfe,
Ys Chryste Jesu
Wythe hys vertu, 35
   Mans soule to be hys wyfe.

Then, love, be trwe,
Come and renewe
   Thyselfe yete onse agayne,
And I shall full swetely 40
Take the to mercye,
   And delyver the owte of payne.

37–8. *These lines are reversed in the MS., but the scribe has placed transposition signs in the margin.*

43

C.U.L., MS. Hh. 4.12, f. 44ᵛ

In the vaile of restles mynd
  I sowght in mownteyn and in mede,
Trustyng a treulofe for to fynd.
  Upon an hyll than toke I hede,
  A voise I herd (and nere I yede)   5
In gret dolour complaynyng tho,
  'See, dere soule, my sydes blede,
Quia amore langueo.'

Upon thys mownt I fand a tree,
  Undir thys tree a man sittyng;   10
From hede to fote wowndyd was he,
  Hys hert blode I saw bledyng,
  A semely man to be a kyng,
A graciose face to loke unto.
  I askyd hym how he had paynyng.   15
He said, '*Quia amore langueo.*

'I am treulove, that fals was never.
  My sister, mannys soule, I loved hyr thus;
Bycause I wold on no wyse dissevere
  I left my kyngdome gloriouse.   20
  I purveyd hyr a paleis preciouse.
She flytt, I folowyd; I luffed her soo
  That I suffred thes paynes piteuouse,
Quia amore langueo.

'My faire love, and my spouse bryght,   25
  I saved hyr fro betyng, and she hath me bett;
I clothed hyr in grace and hevenly lyght,
  This blody surcote she hath on me sett.

For langyng love I will not lett—
Swete strokys be thes, loo!   30
    I haf loved ever als I hett,
Quia amore langueo.

'I crownyd hyr with blysse, and she me with thorne,
    I led hyr to chambre, and she me to dye;
I browght hyr to worship, and she me to skorne,   35
    I dyd hyr reverence, and she me velanye.
    To love that loveth is no maystrye,
Hyr hate made never my love hyr foo—
    Ask than no moo questions whye,
Quia amore langueo.   40

'Loke unto myn handys, man!
    Thes gloves were geven me whan I hyr sowght;
They be nat white, but rede and wan,
    Embrodred with blode (my spouse them bowght!);
    They wyll not of—I lefe them nowght!   45
I wowe hyr with them where ever she goo.
    Thes handes full frendly for hyr fowght,
Quia amore langueo.

'Marvell not, man, thof I sitt styll—
    My love hath shod me wondyr strayte.   50
She boklyd my fete, as was hyr wyll,
    With sharp nailes (well thow maist waite!).
    In my love was never dissaite,
For all my membres I haf opynd hyr to;
    My body I made hyr hertys baite,   55
Quia amore langueo.

'In my syde I haf made hyr nest—
    Loke in me, how wyde a wound is here!—
This is hyr chambre, here shall she rest,
    That she and I may slepe in fere.   60

31 ever] MS. over   39 L. axe me no questioun whi   40 Quia] L.
MS. but quia

42

Here may she wasshe, if any filth were;
Here is socour for all hyr woo.
   Cum if she will, she shall haf chere,
Quia amore langueo.

'I will abide till she be redy,   65
   I will hir sue if she say nay;
If she be rechelesse, I will be redy,
   If she be dawngerouse, I will hyr pray.
   If she do wepe, than byd I nay.
Myn armes ben spred to clypp hyr to.   70
   Crye onys, I cum—now, sowle, assaye!
Quia amore langueo.

'I sitt on an hille for to se farre,
   I loke to the vayle; my spouse I see:
Now rynne she awayward, now cummyth she narre, 75
   Yet fro myn eye-syght she may nat be.
   Sum waite ther pray, to make hyr flee—
I rynne tofore to chastise hyr foo.
   Recover, my soule, agayne to me,
Quia amore langueo.   80

'My swete spouse, will we goo play?
   Apples ben rype in my gardine;
I shall clothe the in new array,
   Thy mete shall be mylk, honye, and wyne.
   Now, dere soule, latt us go dyne;   85
Thy sustenaunce is in my crippe—loo!
   Tary not now, fayre spouse myne,
Quia amore langueo.

'Yf thow be fowle, I shall make clene,
   If thow be seke, I shall the hele;   90
Yf thow owght morne, I shall bemene.
   Spouse, why will thow nowght with me dele?

62 socour] *L.* sete   66 hir sue if] *L.* *MS.* to her send or   67 redy]
L. gredi   77 waite] *MS. corrected from* make   86 crippe] *L.* *MS.* skrypp.

Thow fowndyst never love so lele.
What wilt thow, sowle, that I shall do?
I may of unkyndnes the appele,   95
Quia amore langueo.

'What shall I do now with my spouse?
Abyde I will hyr jantilnesse,
Wold she loke onys owt of hyr howse
    Of flesshely affecciouns and unclennesse!   100
    Hyr bed is made, hyr bolstar is in blysse,
Hyr chambre is chosen—suche ar no moo!
    Loke owt at the wyndows of kyndnesse,
Quia amore langueo.

'My spouse is in hir chambre, hald yowr pease,   105
    Make no noyse, but lat hyr slepe.
My babe shall sofre noo disease,
    I may not here my dere childe wepe,
    For with my pappe I shall hyr kepe.
No wondyr though I tend hyr to—   110
    Thys hoole in my syde had never ben so depe
But *quia amore langueo.*

'Long and love thou never so hygh,
    Yit is my love more than thyn may be.
Thow gladdyst, thow wepist, I sitt the bi.   115
    Yit myght thow, spouse, loke onys at me!
    Spouse, shuld I alway fede the
With childys mete? Nay, love, nat so—
    I preve thi love with adversite,
Quia amore langueo.   120

95 *L.* I may not unkyndeli thee appele   101 *L.* hir bolstir is blis
103 wyndows] *L.* wyndow   105 ff. *This and following stanza in order of L.*
MS. transposes   105 spouse] *L.* love   hir] *L. MS. om.*   113 *L.* longe thou
for love   115 bi] *L. MS.* bygh   116 *L.* yit woldist thou oonys, leef,
loke unto me   119 I preve thi] *MS.* I pray the   *L.* I wole preve

44

'Wax not wery, myn owne dere wyfe!
   What mede is aye to lyffe in counfort?
For in tribulacioun I ryn more ryfe
   Ofter tymes than in disport—
   In welth, in woo, ever I support.   125
Than dere soule, go never me fro!—
   Thy mede is markyd whan thow art mort,
Quia amore langueo.'

44

Hunterian Museum, Glasgow, MS. V.8.15, f.34ʳ

Crist makith to man a fair present,
His blody body with love brent;
That blisful body his lyf hath lent,
For love of man that synne hath blent.

O love, love, what hast thou ment?   5
Me thinketh that love to wratthe is went.

Thi loveliche hondis love hath to-rent,
And thi lithe armes wel streit itent;
Thi brest is baar, thi bodi is bent,
For wrong hath wonne and right is schent.   10

Thi mylde boones love hath to-drawe,
The naylis thi feet han al to-gnawe;
The lord of love love hath now slawe—
Whane love is strong it hath no lawe.

His herte is rent, his body is bent   15
   Upon the roode tre;
Wrong is went, the devel is schent,
   Christ, thurgh the myght of thee.

No. 43. 123 ryn] *L.* regne   126 Than dere soule] *L.* myn owne wijf
128 *Quia*] *L.*   *MS.* in blysse *Quia*
No. 44. 1. makith] *other MSS.* made

45

For thee that herte is leyd to wedde;
Swych was the love that herte us kedde,   20
That herte barst, that herte bledde—
That herte blood oure soulis fedde.

That herte clefte for treuthe of love,
Therfore in him oon is trewe love;
For love of thee that herte is yove—   25
Kepe thou that herte and thou art above.

Love, love, where schalt thou wone?
Thi wonyng-stede is thee binome,
For Cristis herte that was thin hoome,
He is deed—now hast thou noone.   30

Love, love, whi doist thou so?
Love, thou brekist myn herte atwo.

Love hath schewid his greet myght,
For love hath maad of day the nyght;
Love hath slawe the kyng of ryght,   35
And love hath endid the strong fight.

So inliche love was nevere noon;
That witith wel Marie and Joon,
And also witen thei everychon,
That love with hym hath maad at oon.   40

Love makith, Crist, thin herte myn,
So makith love myn herte thin;
Thanne schulde myn be trewe al tym,
And love in love schal make it fyn.

40 hath] *MS. Huntington HM 127   MS.* is

45

C.U.L., MS. Dd.5.64, III, f. 34ᵛ

Lo! lemman swete, now may thou se
That I have lost my lyf for the.
  What myght I do the mare?
Forthi I pray the speciali
That thou forsake ill company   5
  That woundes me so sare;

And take myne armes pryvely
And do tham in thi tresory,
  In what stede sa thou dwelles;
And, swete lemman, forget thow noght   10
That I thi lufe sa dere have boght,
  And I aske the noght elles.

SONGS OF LOVE-LONGING

46

(a)

University College, Oxford, MS. 64 f. 62ᵛ

Jesu be thou my joy, all melody and swetnes,
  And lere me forto synge
  The sange of thi lovynge.

(b)

B.M., MS. Add. 37049, f. 24ʳ

Jesu, my luf, my joy, my reste,
Thi perfite luf close in my breste,
That I the luf and never reste,
And mak me luf the of al thinge best,
And wounde my hert in thi luf fre,   5
That I may reyne in joy evermore with the.

47

47

Jesu, swete is the love of thee,
Noon othir thing so swete may be;
No thing that men may heere and see
Hath no swetnesse ayens thee.

Jesu, no song may be swetter,   5
No thing in herte blisfullere,
Nought may be feelid delitfullere,
Than thou, so sweete a lovere.

Jesu, thi love was us so fre
That it fro hevene broughte thee;   10
For love thou dere boughtist me,
For love thou hynge on roode tre.

Jesu, for love thou tholedist wrong,
Woundis sore, and peynes strong;
Thin peynes weren ful long—   15
No man may hem telle, ne song.

Jesu, for love thou bood so wo
That blody stremys runne the fro;
Thi whyte sydes woxen blw and blo—
Oure synnes it maden so, wolawo!   20

Jesu, for love thou steigh on roode,
For love thou yaf thin herte blode;
Love thee made my soules foode,
Thi love us boughte til al goode.

Jesu, my love, thou were so fre,   25
Al that thou didest for love of me.
What schal I for that yelde thee?
Thou axist nought but love of me.

16 ne song] *MS. Harl. 2253* ne may hem tellen spel ne song

Jesu, my God, Jesu my kyng,
Thou axist me noon othir thing,   30
But trewe love and hert yernyng,
And love-teeris with swete mornyng.

Jesu, my love, Jesu my lyght,
I wole thee love, and that is right;
Do me love thee with al my myght,   35
And for thee moorne bothe day and nyght.

Jesu, do me so yerne thee
That my thought evere upon thee be;
With thin yye loke to me,
And myldely my nede se.   40

Jesu, thi love be al my thought,
Of othir thing ne recche me nought;
Thanne have I thi wille al wrought,
That havest me ful dere bought.

48

Bodl., MS. Digby 86, f. 134ᵛ (col. 1)

Swete Jesu, king of blisse,
Min herte love, min herte lisse,
Thou art swete mid iwisse—
Wo is him that the shal misse.

Swete Jesu, min herte light,   5
Thou art dai withhouten night,
Thou yeve me strengthe and eke might
Forto lovien the al right.

Swete Jesu, mi soule bote,
In min herte thou sette a rote   10
Of thi love that is so swote,
And wite hit that hit springe mote.

No. 47. 33 lyght] *MS.* lygh
No. 48. 6 dai *interlined*

49

49

Bodl., MS. Don. C. 13, f. 166ʳ (col. 1)

Jesu my lefe, Jesu my love, Jesu my covetynge!
To the me langis nyghte and day, thou ert al my joynge.

Jesu, Jesu, Jesu, when wille thou on me rewe?
Bot if I have the love of the, my care is ever newe.

My delite and my hame, Jesu my blisful knynge!   5
Swete ert thou, my swete dreury; in the I hope dwelling.

Ay to dwelle with my lovynge, and play me with my dere,
It thirlis fast in my thynking, and dos me chaunge chere.

Jesu my kynge, I think to the—thou ert sa faire and swete—
Na thing I wil but anely the; heven thou has me hete.   10

Take al my love, hald it with the til I hethin wende;
For the I wil and the I sal love withouten ende.

Al the love that I may love I gife him that me boght;
Ful swete ert thou, my swete Jesu—on the sal be my thoght.

When wil thou com in conforthing, and cover me of care?   15
Forgyve me that I may se—I love the ever mare!

Al mi love is in Jesu, that me langyng has sent;
Thi love me byndis—strenth me thou that me swilk grace has
    lent!

Jesu to synge is mare joyng than any tong may telle;
The myrth to love Jesu above, is na prechour mai spelle.   20

Jesu kinge that made al thing, of a maiden was born,
Help oure hoping and oure lyvyng sa that we be not lorn!

PRAYERS TO CHRIST

50

(a)

BM., MS. Harley 211, f. 147ᵛ

Jesu, that deyed upon a tre
   Owr sowlys for to wynne,
Schilde us from the fendis myght,
   And fro dedly synne.

(b)

N.L.S., MS. Advocates 18.7.21, f. 124ᵛ

Gold and al this werdis wyn
   Is nouht but Cristis rode;
I wolde ben clad in Cristis skyn,
   That ran so longe on blode,
And gon t'is herte and taken myn in—   5
   Ther is a fulsum fode.
Than yef I litel of kith or kyn,
   For ther is alle gode.

51

Merton College, Oxford, MS. 204, f. 208ʳ

Jesu lorde that madest me,
   And with thi blessed blod me boght,
Foryeve that I have greved the
   With word, will, werk, or thought.

No. 50. (b) 2 nouht] *MS.* nouth
No. 51. 2 me boght] *MS.* has me boght   *Other MSS. usually have either* hast/has
or me

Jesu, for thi woundes smert 5
  On foote and on handes two,
Make me meke and low in hert,
  And the to love als I shuld do.

Jesu Criste, to the I call,
  That ert fader ful of myght, 10
Kepe me clene that I ne fall
  In fleshly synne as I have tyght.

Jesu, graunt me myne askyng,
  Perfite paciens in my desese,
And never I mote do that thyng 15
  That shuld the in ony wise displese.

Jesu, that ert heven kyng,
  Sothfast God and man also,
Yeve me grace of good endyng,
  And hem that I am holden to. 20

Jesu, for thi doleful terys
  That thou weptist for my gilt,
Here and spede my prayerys
  And spare me that I be noght spilt.

Jesu, for hem I the beseche 25
  That wrathen thee in ony wise;
Withholde fro hem thine honde of wreche
  And let hem ende in thi servise.

Jesu, joyful for to seen,
  With thi sayntes everychone, 30
Comfort all that careful been,
  And help hem that been wobegone.

10 fader] *MS.* fader god   *other MSS. usually have either* god *or* fader
14 *Some MSS. om.* perfite   15 *Some MSS.* that I make no grucchinge
22 weptist] *Some MSS.* grettest, grat   23 prayerys] *MS.* prayers   25 *above
the stanza the scribe has written* Psalterium caritatis fraterne   26 wrathen]
MS. Lambeth 853 and other MSS.   MS. wrath   28 ende] *other MSS.* lyve
30 With] *other MSS.* of, (un)to   31 all] *other MSS.* hem

52

Jesu, kepe hem that bene goode,
    And mende hem that han greved the,
And send hem frutes and erthly fode,   35
    As eche man nedeth in his degree.

Jesu, that ert withouten lees
    Almyghti God in trinite,
Ceese these werris and send us pees,
    With lastyng love and charite.   40

Jesu, that ert the goostly stoon
    Of all holy chirche in erde,
Bryng thi fooldes flok in oon
    And rule hem with oon herde.

Jesu, for thi blessed bloode,   45
    Bryng tho soules into blys
For whome I have had any goode,
    And spare hem that thei have done amys.

52

Huntington Library, MS. Ellesmere 34.B.7, f. 82^r

O Jesu, lett me never forgett thy byttur passion,
That thou suffred for my transgression,
For in thy blessyd wondes is the verey scole
That must teche me with the worlde to be called a fole.

O Jesu, Jesu, Jesu, grauntt that I may love the soo,   5
That the wysdom of the worlde be cleene fro me agoo,
And brennyngly to desyre to come to see thy face,
In whom is all my comford, my joy, and my solace.

No. 51. 35 hem] *MS. om.* *other MSS.* send hem/men/us   42 in erde]
other MSS. *MS.* the heerde   43 thi fooldes flok] *B.M. Harley Charter 58*
C. 14 *MS.* the fooldes folk   44 herde] *other MSS.* *MS.* hert

(a)

Bodl., MS. Lyell 30, f. 15ᵛ

Jesu Crist, my soule leche,
  That didest on the rode tree,
With al myn hert I the byseche
  Al my synnys foryeve me,
And evermore in hert myn   5
  Let thi passion fastned be,
As was the spere into thyn
  When thow suffredest deth for me.

(b)

Bodl. MS. Rawl. Liturg. f. 36, f. 63ᵛ

Jesu, for thy holy name
And for thy bitter passion,
Save us fro synne and shame,
And endles dampnacion. . . .

(c)

Bodl. MS. Lyell 30, f. 285ᵛ

Jesu, for thi blysfull blod,
  Bryng thoo soulus into thi blys
Of whom I have had eny good,
  And spare that thei have doon amys.

(d)

C.U.L., MS. Ii. 6.2, f. 107ᵛ

O Jesu, lorde, wellcum thou be,
In forme of brede as y the se;
O Jesu, for thy holy name,
Schelde me thys day from sorro and schame,

And lete me lyfe in trewth and ryght,   5
Before my dethe hafe hosyll and schryfte;
O Jesu, as thou were of a mayden borne,
Let me never be forlorne;
And let me never for no syne
Lese the blysse that thou art in.   10

(e)

Bodl. MS. Digby 86, f. 206ʳ

In thine honden, loverd mine,
I biteche soule mine;
Sothfast God, bidde I the,
That mine sunen foryef thou me.

54

Bodl. MS. Bodley 789, f. 148ʳ

	Jesu, for thi precious blood,	
	That thou schaddist for oure good	
	In thi circumcision	
Luxuria	Ayens the synne of leccherie,	
	Kepe us, lord, fro that synne,	5
	Bringe hem out that beth therynne,	
	Save us all from dampnacioun,	
Castitas	And kepe us in clennesse of chastite.	
	Pater noster and Ave.	

	Jesu, for thi precious blood,	
	That thou schaddist for oure good	10
	In the mounte of Oliveet,	
	Whanne thou were with scourgis beete,	
Gula	Ayens the synne of glotonie,	
	Kepe us, lord, fro that synne,	
	Delyvere hem out that ben therynne,	15

No. 53. (e). 3 God] *MS.* goed

Abstinencia	And hold us in the vertu of abstinence. Pater noster and ave.

Jesu, for thi precious blood,
That thou schaddist for oure good
Out of thi blesside heed,
That with a corowne of thornes was biweved,   20
Longe, scharpe, and kene,

Superbia   Ayens the synne of pride,
Schilde us alle fro that synne,
Delyvere hem out that ben therynne,

Humilitas   And kep us alle in meeknesse clene.   25
Pater noster and Ave.

Jesu, for thi precious blood,
That thou schaddist for our good
Out of thi right honde

Ira   Ayens the synne of wraththe,
Kepe us, lord, fro that synne,   30
Brynge hem out that ben therinne,

Paciencia   And holde us in the vertu of pacience.
Pater noster and Ave.

Jesu, for thi precious blood,
That thu schaddist for oure good
Out of thi lift hond,   35

Cupiditas   Ayens the synne of coveitise,
Schilde us, lord, fro that synne,
Delyvere hem out that ben therynne,

Elemosina   And kepe us in largenesse of werkis of merci.
Pater noster and Ave.

Jesu, for thi precious blood,   40
That thou schaddist for oure good
Out of bothe thi feet,

Ociositas   Ayens the synne of sleuthe,
Schilde us alle fro that synne
Brynge hem out that ben therynne,   45

Occupacio	And kepe us in good occupacioun.
	Pater noster and Ave Maria.

Jesu, for thi precious blood,
That thou schaddist for oure good,
Out of thi blesside herte,

Invidia   Ayens the synne of envye,   50
Schilde us, lord, fro that synne,
Delyvere hem out that ben therynne,

Caritas   And kep us in parfijt charite.

Jesu, for thi woundis wide,
With thi meeknesse fordo my pride,   55
And all yvel that mai me bitide.
Amen, for charite.
    Pater noster, Ave, and Credo.

PRAYERS AND POEMS TO THE
VIRGIN MARY

55

Magdalen College, Oxford, MS. 60, f. 214^r

At a sprynge-wel under a thorn,
Ther was bote of bale
A lytel here aforn;
Ther bysyde stant a mayde,
Fulle of love ybounde.
Hoso wol seche trwe love,
Yn hyr hyt schal be founde.

Trinity College, Cambridge, MS. 323, f. 42ᵛ

Levedie, ic thonke the
   Wid herte suithe milde
That god that thou havest idon me
   Wid thine suete childe.

Thou ard god and suete and briht,   5
   Of alle otheir icoren;
Of the was that suete wiht
   That was Jesus iboren.

Maide milde, biddi the
   Wid thine suete childe   10
That thou erndie me
   To habben Godis milce.

Moder, loke one me
   Wid thine suete eye:
Reste and blisse gef thou me,   15
   Mi levedi, then ic deye.

57

Bodl. MS. Rawl. poet. 34, f. 18ᵛ

Away, feyntt lufe, full of varyaunce!
   Mych flateryng thow hast, and lytyl trust!
I forsake all thy daliaunce:
   Syth thou arte weddyd to luste,
   Another lady chese me muste,   5
Wich evermore ys perseveraunt
In luff, and never varyaunt.

No. 56. 3 god] *MS.* gohid   5, 7 briht, wiht] *MS.* brit, wist   6 icoren]
MS. icorinne   11 erndie] *MS.* herdie   14, 16 eye, deye] *MS.* eþen,
deþen   15 gef] *MS.* ges   16 levedi *corrected from* lehedi

But wher schall I that lady fynde,
  That never wyll fro me owttrage?
Syche one were off a noble kynde,   10
  Lyke as in youthe, so loffyng in age;
  Iwysse, that lady wyll yiff corage
Unto here luffer for to be trewe,
And never to chaunge her for no new.

Throwowte thys wordle I wolle hyr seche   15
  Both north and sowth, by est and west,
To spend my labur and my spech
  And doe my dylygence to love hyr best—
  Then myght my herte be sette in rest,
That hath soe long tyme luffyd in vayn,   20
And fyndyth no stedfast luff agayn.

None erthly tresure wold I compayr,
  Gold, sylver, nor precious stone,
No woman, wer sche never so feyre,
  Owther high of byrth, unto such one—   25
  For sych a lady I make my mone,
Wich only I chese to paramour,
And synguler leche of my doloure.

Par case sche be off hygh degre,
  And I off lowe and pouer estate,   30
Yyit if fortune my frend wyll be,
  I may her wyn, other erly or late.
  I have knowyn sum so fortunate,
Wych though they wer ful lowe of kyn,
Kyngys doghtyrs by grace dyd wyn.   35

And so I myght by grace atteyn,
  Unto here lufe, that were most hygh.
Yf at the bygynnyng sche wold dysdeyne,
  Yitt vertuus gydyng myght bryng me nyghe.

30 And I off] *MS.* And off   32 erly] *MS.* erthly

59

Gode lady, for thy luff I syghe,   40
That nothyng may doe me no plesaunce,
Butt only thy remembraunse.

Wherfor, in thy memoryall,
    Myne herte thyn herbere wyl I make;
Among all herbys grett and smale,   45
    Pentafiloun therto schall be take—
    It hath v. levys, wich for thy sake
Schall be enamelyd with the same
Fyve lettrys conteynid in thy name.

M. for most meke maydyn and mother,   50
    Fyguryd in Mychell, a lady of Israell,
Fyrst spowse, icheece afor all other,
    To David, as doth the story tell.
    Of mercy called sche ys the well,
To whome, evermore immaculate,   55
The margarite is well appropriate.

A. for the wyff of Naball, Abigaill,
    Inprudente als Adam withoute avisement,
Answeryng David, wherfor he wold hym kyll,   59
    But by the prudence of Abigaill chaunged hys entent.
    My lady in fygure as the adamauntt, to whom was lent
Propyrte attractyff, when sche seyde,
'Loo', mekly, 'my lordes own handemayde!'

R. for Rachel, withowtt deformyte,
    Crunyd with the ruby off schamefastnes,   65
Example to woman in ych degre
    Off wommanhode, vertu, and lowlynes,
    Modyr to Joseph, innocent, as doth wytnes
The fyrst boke off the old testament,
Wych fygure to my lady is convenyent.   70

60 chaunged] *MS.* chunged   65 Crunyd] *MS.* curndyd

60

I. for Judith, that lady vyctoryus,
   Wych thurgh her meknes and chastyte
In her gyding as the jaspid was gracius,
   That the Juery sche savyd fro captyvite.
   O lady Judith, that ever durst ye   75
   Prynce Olyfern with yowre handes kyll,
In fygure off my lady, yt was Goddes wyll!

A. knyttyth thys conclucion
   Upon my soverayn lades name,
To whom withowte abusion   80
   Is fygure a lady of grete fame,
   Abisaag, with allatory, wich men fro blame
Preservyth, and procuryth benyvolence
Off soverayn to servunt ayenst offence.

Who lykyth to wytt more plenerly   85
   Whatt that I mene in thys processe,
The Bybill and the lapydary for to study
   Let them converte her besynesse,
   In the herball also, fyve-levyd gresse,
What propyrtees yt hath yf thow wyll rede,   90
Off the mystery son may thow spede.

For I have purposyd in my mynde
   My soverayn lady for to hyde
In fygure of scrypture as I hur fynde,
   For whom all other be putt asyde,   95
   Unto whos grace good God me gyde,
That may all bale turn into blysse—
Loo, such my soverayn yss!

                   [Lenvoy]

Go, lytill balett, and doe me recommende
   Unto my lady with godely countynaunce,   100
Bysekyng hur that sche me sende
   Comfortt ayenst all comberaunce,

75 ye] *MS.* Sche   90 thow] *MS.* the   92 mynde] *MS.* mende

61

And me deffend from all myschaunce,
So that afore my fyniall howr
I may hur see to my succour.   105

58

Bodl., MS. e Mus. 23, p. 162

Hayle, flowre of vyrgynyte!
In hevyn thou haste pryncypalite
   With worschyppys and honowre:
Thy blysse is more in dygnyte
Than all seyntes that evyr schall be   5
   Or angelis yn hevyn bowre.

59

C.U.L., MS. Ee. 1.12, f. 78ᵛ

O emperesse, the emperoure
   Quem meruisti portare,
Of heven and erthe hath made the floure:
   Regina celi, letare!

O quene of grace, the king of blisse   5
   Quem meruisti portare,
Hath made thy sete next unto his:
   Regina celi, letare!

O princesse pure, the prince of peas,
   Quem meruisti portare,   10
Ever thy joye he doth encreas:
   Regina celi, letare!

O lady fre, the lorde of alle,
   Quem meruisti portare
Hath made man free, that was moost thralle: 15
   Regina celi, letare!

O swete moder, thy sone Jesus,
   Quem meruisti portare,
He rose ayene, that died for us:
   Regina celi, letare!   20

O mayden myelde, thy sone so dere,
   Quem meruisti portare,
Hath crowned the in blis so clere:
   Regina celi, letare!

O spowse of Criest, oure savyoure,   25
   Quem meruisti portare,
Heven and erthe the doth honoure:
   Regina celi, letare!

O Marie, of thy sonne aske this,
   Quem meruisti portare,   30
That we may dwelle with him and his:
   Regina celi, letare!

60

B.M., MS. Cotton Caligula A. II, f. 107ᵛ

Surge, mea sponsa, so swete in syghte,
   And se thy sone in sete full shene!
Thow shalt abyde with thy babe so bryghte
   And in my glorye be, and be called a qwene.
Thy mamelles, modur, full well I mene,   5
     I hadde to my mete, I myghte not mysse.
Above all creatures, my modur clene,
   Veni coronaberis.

Cum, clene crystall, to my cage,
   Columba mea, I the calle!   10
And se thy sone that in servage
   For mannus sowle was made thralle.

No. 60. 4 called] *MS. Harley 2251* crowned   9 clene] *MS. Lambeth 853*
clenner than my] *H.* thy   11 that] *H., L. MS.* sone in

63

In thy place that ys princypall
  I playde pryvely wythowte mysse;
Myn high cage, modur, have thou shall,   15
    Veni coronaberis.

For macula, modur, was nevur in the,
  Filia Syon, thou art the flowre!
Full swetely shalte thou sytte by me,
  And were a crowne wyth me in towre;   20
  And all myn angelles to thyn honowre
    Shall the worshyppe in heven blysse.
  Thow, blessed body that me bare in bowre,
    Veni coronaberis.

Tota pulchra es to my plesynge,   25
  My modur, princes of Paradys!
A watur full swete of the shall sprynge—
  Thow shalt ayeyn my ryghtes ryse.
  The welle of mercy, modur, in the lyys
    To brynge thy blessed body to blysse,   30
  And all my sayntes shall do the servysse,
    Veni coronaberis.

Veni, electa mea, to myn an hyye,
  Holy modur and mayden mylde,
On sege to sytte me bye,   35
  That am thy kynge and thy chylde,
  Holy modur, with me to bylde,
    Wyth thy blessed babe that ys in blysse—
  That virgyn that was nevur defylde,
    Veni coronaberis.   40

13 place that ys] *L.* palijs so   15 Myn high cage] *L., H. MS.* herytage
21 angelles] *H., L.* seyntes   23 Thow] *H., L.* that me] *H., L. MS* that
bare   27 *L.* of the a watir ful weel gan sprynge   28 *L.* that schal ayen
alle my rightis rise *H.* that often tyme of the shal rise   33 to myn an hyye]
L. meekeli chosen *H. om. this stanza*   35 *L.* On sege to sitte semeli bi him
an hiʒ

Vox tua to me was full swete
  Whene thou me badde, 'babe be stylle',
Full goodly gone oure lyppes mete,
  Wyth bryghte braunches, as blosme on hyll.
  Favus distillans that wente wyth wylle   45
    Oute of thy lyppes whene we dede kysse.
  Therfore, modure, thys ys my skyll:
    Veni coronaberis.

Veni de Libano, thou lylye in launche,
  That lapped me lovely wyth lullynge songe,   50
Thow shalte abyde wyth thy blessed braunche
  That so solemply of the spronge.
  Ego, flos campy, thy flowre, was fonge,
    That on Calverye cryede to the, ywysse.
  Moder, ye knowe hyt ys no wronge,   55
    Veni coronaberis.

Pulchra ut luna, thou bere the lambe,
  As soune that shyneth moste clere.
Veni in ortum meum, thowghty damme,
  To smelle my spyces and erbes in fere.   60
  My place ys pyghte for the plenere,
    Full of bryghte braunches and blomes of blysse.
  Cum now, modur, to thy derlynge dere,
    Veni coronaberis.

Que est ista so vertuus,   65
  That is celestyall for her mekenesse?
Aurora consurgens gracyous,
  So benygne a lady of fyne bryghtnesse,
  That ys the colour of kynde clennesse,
    Regina celi, that nevur shall mysse.   70
  Thus endeth thys songe of gret swettenesse,
    Veni coronaberis.

44 *H.* with braunchis and flouris of swete smelle   46 thy] *L.* oure   *H.* oure
mowth betwene   47 skyll] *H* . . . it was my wille   *L.* now ful stille
50 lapped] *MS.* lappes   *L.* lappid   *H.* lapidius   52 solemply] *L.* semeli
57 bere] *H., L.* berist   lambe] *H.* name   66 her] *MS.* oure   *L.* that is
evere lastyng for her meekenes   71 endeth] *MS.* entheth

65

Bodl. MS. Douce 322, f. 8ᵛ

In a tabernacle of a toure,
   As I stode musyng on the mone,
A crouned quene, most of honoure,
   Apered in gostly syght ful sone.
   She made compleynt thus by hyr one   5
      For mannes soule was wrapped in wo:
   'I may nat leve mankynde allone,
      Quia amore langueo.

'I longe for love of man my brother,
   I am hys vokete to voyde hys vyce;   10
I am his mediatryce and his moder—
   Why shuld I my dere chylde dispyce?
   Yef he me wrathe in diverse wyse,
      Through flesshes freelte fall me fro,
   Yet bus me rewe to he wil ryse   15
      Quia amore langueo.

'I byd, I byde in grete longyng,
   I love, I loke when man woll crave,
I pleyne for pyte of peynyng;
   Wolde he aske mercy, he shuld hit have.   20
   Say to me, soule, and I shall save;
      Byd me, my barne, and I shall go;
   Thow prayde me never but my son forgave,
      Quia amore langueo.

'O wreche in the worlde, I loke on the,   25
   I se thy trespas day by day,
With lechery ageyns my chastite,
   With pryde agene my pore aray;

2 musyng] *Add. 37049, Rawl. C 86* musand(e)   4 *Add.* I sawe syttyng
(*Rawl.* sittande) on a trone   11 *Add., as conj. Riddy* *MS.* I am hys moder
I can none other   14 Through] *MS.* though   flesshes freelte] *varr. incl.*
fleschly frellte (lysk), freelte of flesshe   15 bus . . . ryse] *Add.* (*Riddy*)
MS. must we (*Rawl.* it must me) rewe hym tyll   22 barne] *Add.* (*Riddy*).
Cf. Paris, Bibl. nat. MS. angl. 41 barun   *MS.* chylde

My love abydes, thyne ys away;
  My love the calles, thow steles me fro;   30
Sewe to me, synner, I the pray,
    Quia amore langueo.

'Moder of mercy I was for the made;
  Who nedys it, man, but thow allone?
To gete the grace I am more glade   35
  Than thow to aske hit—why wil thou noon?
  When seyd I nay, tel me, tyll oon?
    Forsoth never yet to frende ne foo!
  When thou askes nought, than make I moone,
    Quia amore langueo.   40

'I seke the in wele and wrechednesse,
  I seke the in ryches and poverte;
Than, man, beholde where thy moder ys,
  Why loves thou me nat syth I love the?
  Synful or sory how evere thow be,   45
    So welcome to me there ar no mo;
  I am thy suster, trust on me,
    Quia amore langueo.

'My childe ys outlawed for thy synne,
  My barne ys bette for thy trespasse;   50
Yt prykkes myne hert that so ny my kynne
  Shuld be dysseased. O sone, allasse!
  Thow art hys brother, thy moder I was;
    Thow sokyd my pappe, thow lovyd man so;
  Thow dyed for hym, myne hert thow has,   55
    Quia amore langueo.

29–30 abydes . . . calles . . . steles] *Add.* abydes . . . cals . . . stels *MS.* abydeth
. . . calleth . . . stelest   31 Sewe] *MS.* shewe   34 nedys it, man] *as
conj. Riddy Add.* nedys it none,   *Douce 78* nedithe hit man   *MS.* nedeth hit but
35 gete] *most MSS.* geve   36 wil] *Add. MS.* wylt   39 askes] *Add.
MS.* askest   43 Than] *Add. MS.* Thow   44 loves] *Add.* lufs *MS.* lovest
47 trust] *Douce 78* tryste *MS.* ryght trust   50 barne . . . thy] *Add.*
MS. mankynde . . . hys *cf. Rawl.* my childe   51 Yt prykkes] *as conj. Riddy
Add.* It prykkes *Rawl.*yt *MS.* yet prykketh   53 thy] *Add., Rawl. MS.* hys
55 thow] *Add. MS.* he

'Man, leve thy synne than for my sake;
  Why shulde I gyf the that thou nat wald?
And yef thow synne, som prayere take,
  And trust in me as I have tald   60
  Am nat I thy moder called?
    Why shulde thou flee? I love the—loo,
  I am thy frende, I helpe—behald,
    Quia amore langueo.'

'Now sone,' she sayde, 'wil thou sey nay,   65
  Whan man wolde mende hym of hys mys?
Thow lete me never in veyne yet pray.
  Than, synfull man, see thow to thys—
  What day thou comes, welcome thow ys,
    Thys hundreth yere yef thow were me fro;   70
  I take the ful fayne, I clyppe, I kysse,
    Quia amore langueo.

'Now wol I syt and sey nomore,
  Leve, and loke with grete longyng,
Whan man woll calle, I wol restore;   75
  I love to save hym—he ys myne osprynge;
  No wonder yef myne hert on hym hynge,
    He ys my neyghbore; what may I doo?
  For hym have I thys worshippyng,
    And therefore *amore langueo.*   80

'Why was I crouned and made a quene?
  Why was I called of mercy the welle?
Why shuld an erthly woman bene
  So hygh in heven above aungelle?
  For the, mankynde—the truthe I telle!   85
    Than aske mercy, and I shall do
  That I was ordeyned, helpe the fro helle,
    Quia amore langueo.

58–63 wald, tald, behald] *Add. MS.* wolde, tolde, beholde   59 yef] *MS.*
yet yef   60 And] *Add., etc. MS.* or   62 thou flee] *Add. MS.* I flee the
65 wil] *Add. MS.* wylt   69 comes] *MS.* comest   70 me fro] *MS.* fro
Add., Rawl.   78, 79, ys, have] *Add., as conj. Riddy MS* was, had   86 Than]
Rawl. (Riddy) MS. thou   86–7 mercy, helpe] *Add. (Riddy) MS.* me helpe, kepe.

'Nowe, man, have mynde on me forever,
  Loke on thy love thus languysshyng;   90
Late us never fro other dissevere,
  Myne helpe ys thyne oune, crepe under my wynge;
  Thy syster ys a quene, thy brother a kynge,
    Thys heritage ys tayled—sone, come therto,
  Take me for thy wyfe and lerne to synge,   95
    Quia amore langueo.'

62

B.M., MS. Arundel 285, f. 196ᵛ

Haill! quene of hevin, and steren of blis;
Sen that thi sone thi fader is,
How suld he ony thing the warn,
And thou his mothir, and he thi barne?

Haill! fresche fontane that springis new,   5
The rute and crope of all vertu,
Thou polist gem without offence,
Thou bair the lambe of innocence.

63

Lambeth Palace, MS. 853, p. 24

Heil be thou, Marie, the modir of Crist,
  Heil, the blessidist that evere bare child!
Heil, that conceyvedist al with list
  The sone of God bothe meeke and mylde!
  Heil, maiden sweete that nevere was filid!   5
    Heil, welle of witt and al wijsdome!
  Heil, thou flour! Heil, fairest in feeld!
    Ave regina celorum!

No. 61. 90 thus] *MS.* thys   93 brother] *Douce 78   MS.* brother ys
  No. 63. 5 maiden] *MSS. Balliol 354, Adv. 19.3.1   MS.* maide   6 *MS.* heil
welle and witt of al wijsdome   *Cf. B.* hayle well, hayle wyte of all wysedome

Heil, comeli queene, coumfort of care!
  Heil, blessid lady bothe fair and bright!   10
Heil, the salvour of al sare!
  Heil, the laumpe of lemys light!
  Heil, thou blessid beerde, in the was pight
    The joie of man bothe al and sum!
  Heil, pinacle in hevene an hight,   15
    Mater regis angelorum!

Heil, crowned queene, fairest of alle!
  Heil, that alle oure blis in bredde!
Heil, that alle wommen on doon calle
  In temynge whanne thei ben hard bistedde!   20
  Heil, thou that alle feendis dredde,
    And schul do til the day of doome!
  With maidens mylk thi sone thou fedde,
    O Maria, flos virginum!

Heil, fairest that evere God fand,   25
  Whiche chees thee to his owne bour!
Heil, the lanterne that is ay lightand
  To hye and lowe, to riche and poure!
  Heil, spice swettist of savour!
    Heil, that al oure joye of come!   30
  Heil, of alle wommen fruyt and flour,
    Velud rosa vel lilium!

Heil be thow, goodli ground of grace!
  Heil, blessid sterre upon the see!
Heil be thou, comfort in every caas!   35
  Heil, the cheevest of charitee!

11 salvour] *B.* heler *Adv.* socure *MS. Trin. Coll. Dublin 516* salve   sare]
MS. sore   12 of]*B., Adv.* that   13 the] *other MSS.* *MS.* whom
14 the] *B., Adv.* *MS.* heil   18 bredde] *MS.* bradde   20 In temynge]
Adv. when thei with chylde   *B.* and namly   *T.C.D.* altyme that   bistedde]
MS. bistadde   22 schul] *T.C.D.* *MS.* schulen *B., Adv.* shall   25, 27 fand,
lightand] *MS.* foond, lightond   28 *from Adv.* (*so other MSS.*)   *MS.* to thee
schulen loute bothe riche and poore   35 be thou, comfort] *B.* *MS.* of
coumfortis   36 charitee] *T.C.D.* *B., Adv.* chastite

Heil, welle of witt and of merci!
    Heil, that bare Jesu, Goddes sone!
Heil, tabernacle of the trynyte,
        Funde preces ad filium!   40

Heil be thow, virgyne of virgins!
    Heil, blessid modir! Heil, blessid may!
Heil, norische of sweete Jesus!
    Heil, cheefest of chastite! as thou wele may,
    Lady, kepe us so in oure last day   45
        That we may come to his kingdom.
    For me and alle cristen thou pray,
        Pro salute fidelium.

64

Bodl., MS. Lyell 30, f. 176ʳ

O lady, sterre of Jacob, glorie of Israel,
    Of all blessid, O blessedist virgine,
For thylke tydyng which that Gabriel
    Broght to the, most hevenly and devine,
    So lat thi stremes of grace upon me shyne,   5
And of thine yen the merciable lyght
Fro all myscheff to save me this nyght.

O feyrist doghtur of Jerusalem,
    Flour of all flourus, O flour of chastite!
For thilke joy thou haddist in Bedlem   10
    Of blessid Jesu in the nativite,
    Visited aftur of worthi kyngis thre,
Of wheche gladnes devoutely remembryng,
Save me this nyght, slepyng and wakyng.

No. 63. 38 Goddes sone] *Adv.* god of heyvun   *B.* highest in hevyns blome
T.C.D. al and sum   41 virgins] *B.*, *Adv.*   *T.C.D.* vertues   44 as thou
wele may] *Adv.* *MS.* forsothe to say   45 *B.*, *T.C.D.* to thi sone thou say
Adv. heyle he lady to thi sone thou prey   46 his] *B.*, *Adv.*, *T.C.D.* *MS.* thi
No. 64. 14 Save] *MS.* gave

And for that joy of sovereyne dignite   15
   Which folowid aftur thi sones passion,
When through his ryal divine majeste,
   Callid by prophetis of Juda the lyon,
   Wheche made fro deth his resurreccion,
For the grete gladnes thou haddist on that morow   20
Kepe me this nyght fro all myscheff and sorow.

And for the joy thou haddist evermore,
   A joy precellyng in comparison,
When he of mercy, mankynde to restore,
   Toward that hevenly sterrid mansion   25
   Made in oure manhode his ascension,
For which joy, O princes, I the prey,
Kepe me this nyght that no fende me werreie.

And for that joy surmountyng joyes all
   Which that thou haddist in thyn assumpcion,   30
When thou were crouned in that hevenly stall,
   Quene of all quenis, moost sovereyne of renoun,
   Reseyve thi servant undur thi proteccion,
This nyght and ever, pavis of my defens,
Which flitth for socour to thi magnificens.   35

And to remembre thi famous joyes fyve,
   To myn availe and my gret avauntage,
Undur thi support, while that I am alyve,
   I shall uche a nyght with umul and mekhe visage,
   Knelyng afore the in maner of homage,   40
Thi joyes remembryng, and after, surly slepe,
Fro all asautus while ye lust me to kepe.

Moost holy princes, moost gracious and benygne,
   And of mercy moost plentevous and abounde,
Set thi fyve joyes for a speciall signe   45
   Afore myn hert, to abyde ther and rebounde,

26 Made] *MS*. and made   28 werreie] *MS*. werrie

72

In every myscheff that hit may be founde,
While I thi servant have hem in remembraunce,
Ayeyne goostly enemyes to stonde in assurauns.

65

Victoria and Albert Museum, MS. Reid 7, f. 2ᵛ

> The stern of heven, modre Marye,
>   That with hir mylke fed Cryst Jesu,
> Of deth that Adam folily
>   Had plantid, she the roote up dreu.
>
> That same stern, wochsave she now   5
>   The sterns above to stil and pees,
> Whose stryfe and batailles as is to trow
>   Arn cause of folkes dedely dissees.

PRAYERS TO SAINTS AND THE
GUARDIAN ANGEL

66

Fitzwilliam Museum, Cambridge, MS. 40–1950, f. 107ᵛ

> Jesu, whom ye serve dayly,
> Uppon your enemys gyff you victory;
> Off the holy crosse the vertu
> Your gode fortune alwey renew;
> Oure Lady and Saynt Gabryell   5
> Geve you long lyffe and gode hele;
> And Saynt George, the gode knyght,
> Over your fomen geve you myght;
> And holy Saynt Kateryne
> To youre begynnyng send gode fyne;   10
> Saynt Christofre, botefull on see and lond,
> Joyfully make you see Englond!

67

B.M., MS. Harley 667, f. 100ᵛ

Seint Marie Magdalene, lady fair and bright,
Al Crestendam clere thoroth thi gostly light;
Thow techest men to leve syne and love God on right;
To them that thi helpe bysek kithe thi mekul myght.

Seint Mari Magdalene, thi grace be ful ryve;   5
Mani man has thou delivered of prisone and of gyfe,
Oft of alle sekenesse, and ded folk brouht to live:
To my nede think on me, and my help sped blive.

Seint Marie Magdalene, I mak to the my mone;
I am synful—me nede thi help befor Godes trone.   10
Off them that thou willt defend ther be dampned none—
I besek, kithe that on me and on my frendes ilkone.

68

C.U.L., MS. Ee. 1.12, f. 79ʳ

Hayle! holy father of the high cuntrey,
  Of frere mynours the beawtie and light,
Of a just man the rightfull wey,
  Of goode maners the rule moost right:
  By thy vertu and goostely myght,   5
Out of this lyfe when we shull wende,
To blisse lede us that hath noon ende.

69

Ushaw College, Durham, MS. 10, f 1ʳ

O blyssyd kynge, so full of vertue,
  The flowr of all knyghthod that never was fylyd,
Thou pray for us to Criste Jesu,
  And to hys modyr, Mary myld;

No. 67. 1–4 bright, light, right, myght] *MS.* brithg, lithg, *etc.*   3 techest]
MS. th thcest

In all thi warkys thou was never wyld,   5
    Bott full of grace and of charyte,
Mercyfull ever to man and chylde—
    Now, sweyt kyng Henre, pray for me.

O crownyd kyng with sceptur in hand,
    Most nobyll conqueror I may the call,   10
For thou hast conqueryd, I undyrstand,
    A hevynly kyngdome most imperyall
    Hwar joye abundeth and grace perpetuell
        In presens of the holy Trenite,
    Off wych grace thou make me parcyall—   15
        Now, swet Kyng Henre, praye for me.

All apostels and patriarchs schall the honor,
    Martyrs and confessors with all ther delygens,
And eke virgynes in the hevynly towr
    Ar glad and joyfull of thi presens;   20
    Angelys and Archangelys with ample reverence
        Schall mynystyr and (giftes?) bryng to the,
    The well of pety and of pacyens—
        Now, swet kyng Henre, praye for me.

Thy prayer I trust is hard in hevyn   25
    With the Fadyr omnipotent;
Now blyssyd be thy name to newyne,
    For ever att neyd thou art present;
    In trowbyll or payn wen I am schent
        Or standde in wardly juberte   30
    Thy socur to me full son thou sentt—
        Now, sweyt kyng Henre, praye for me.

Thy trowbulas lyf and grett vexacion
    With pacyens that thou had therein,
And thi constans in contemplacion   35
    Has mad the hevyn for to wyne;

22] *MS. very faded*

Thy sett is ordenyd with seraphyn
   As langhyght to thi regalyte
With mor melody then I can myn—
   Now, swet kyng Henre, praye for me.　　　　40

O blessyd kyng so gracyos and gud,
   Thou pray to sett this reme in rest
Unto owr saveyowr that dyed on roud,
   And to hys modyr, that madyn blessyd,
   That alkyn wrangys may be redressyd　　　45
      To plesor of the deyte,
   Thys I besech at my request—
      Now, swet kyng Henre, praye for me.

70

Balliol College, Oxford, MS. 354, f. 144ʳ

O angell dere, wher ever I goo,
   Me that am commytted to thyn awarde,
Save, defende, and govern also,
   That in hewyn with the be my reward.

Clense my sowle from syn that I have do,　　　5
   And vertuosly me wysse to Godward;
Shyld me from the fende evermo,
   And fro the peynes of hell so hard.

O thou cumly angell, so gud and clere,
   That ever art abydyng with me,　　　　10
Thowgh I may nother the se nor here,
   Yet devoutely with trust I pray to the.

My body and sowle thou kepe in fere,
   With soden deth departid that they not be,
For that ys thyn offes, both fere and nere,　　　15
   In every place wher ever I be.

No. 70. 12 I pray] MS. I the pray *with* the *crossed through*

76

O blessid angell, to me so dere,
  Messangere of God almyght,
Govern my dedis and thowght in fere,
  To the plesaunce of God, both day and nyght.   20

MYSTERIES OF THE FAITH

71

Bodl., MS. Laud misc. 108, f. 238ᵛ

Byhalde merveylis: a mayde ys moder,
Her sone her fader ys and broder;
Lyfe faught with dethe and dethe is slayne;
Most high was lowe—he styghe agayne.

72

Bodl., MS. Rawlinson B 332, f. iiᵛ

A God, and yet a man?
  A mayde, and yet a mother?
Witt wonders what witt can
  Conceave this or the other.

A God, and can he die?   5
  A dead man, can he live?
What witt can well replie?
  What reason reason give?

God, Truth it selfe doth teache it;
  Mans witt sinkes too farr under,   10
By reasons power to reach it—
  Beleeve, and leave to wonder.

73

Hore Beate Marie Virginis (1514)

God be in my heed,
And in myn understandynge;
God be in myn eyen,
And in my lokynge;
God be in my mouthe,   5
And in my spekynge;
God be in my herte,
And in my thynkynge;
God be at myn ende,
And my departynge.   10

74

xx songes (1530)

Pleasure yt ys
To here iwys
  The byrdes synge;
The dere in the dale,
The shepe in the vale,   5
  The corne spryngyng.

Gods purvyaunce
For sustenaunce
  Yt ys for man;
Then we allwayse   10
To hym give prase
  And thank hym than.

No. 74. 3 byrdes] *text* byrds

75

B.M., MS. Add. 34193, f. 119ᵛ

The gladsom byrd, the deys mesanger,
  Synggyng with musicall armonye,
Sayth in hys song the dey gynneth to clere,
  And byddyth us adressone us and hye
  Toward the lyff, the lyf that schall not dye;   5
Thys is the voyce ryght of the byrd of blys,
Syngynge tyll us that the dey cummyng is.

Thys byddyth this heyvynly pursyvant,
  That we schuld all from slomoryng aryse,
And that we schuld bene holly attendaunt   10
  To plesen Godd devotly with service;
  Ryghtwos and chast and eke in sobre wyse,
The lyght of grace is drawyng tyll us nere
Of owr derknes the clowdes for to clere.

76

Bodl., MS. Eng. poet. e. 1, f. 16ʳ

Now is wele and all thing aright,
And Cryst ys come as a trew knyght,
For owr broder ys kyng of myght,
  The fend to fleme and all his—
Thus the feend ys put to flyght,   5
  And all his boost abatyd ys.

Sythyn yt is wele, wele we do,
For there ys none but one of two,
Hevyn to gete, or hevyn forgo;
  Oder mene non there ys—   10
I counsayll you, syn yt ys so,
  That ye wele do to wyn you blys.

No. 76. 7 *MS*. Sythyn yt is we wele we do   10 mene] *MS*. men
12 wele] *MS*. wyll

Now ys well and all ys wele,
   And ryght wele, so have y bliss;
And sythyn all thyng ys so well,   15
   I rede we do no more amiss.

PENITENCE AND THE CHRISTIAN LIFE

77

(a)

B.M., MS. Harley 5398, f. 20ʳ

Goddys chosyn who so wil be,
   And ever wony on his blis,
Of viii rosis then most he
   A glorious garlond make ywis:

Thynk al thi gilte, Ofte hit wepe,   5
   Wil do no more, Thyn enemy thou love,
Thynk on thy deth, Drede paynes depe,
   Aske mercy, Have blis above.

(b)

Bodl., MS. Laud Misc. 213, f. 2ᵛ

The fende oure foo may not us dere
Bot we boghen to hym for fere:
He ys a lyoun but thou withstonde,
Not worth a flye yf thou ne wonde.

78

Bodl. MS. Douce 104, f. 112ᵛ

Tutivillus, the devyl of hell,
He wryteth har names, sothe to tel,
   Ad missam garulantes.

No. 78. *The edge of the MS. page is badly faded, and the Latin lines are almost illegible*

Better wer be attome for ay
Than her to serve the devil to pay, 5
   Sic vana famulantes.

Thes women that sitteth the church about,
Thei beth al of the develis rowte,
   Divina impedientes.

But thai be stil, he wil ham quell, 10
With kene crokes draw hem to hell,
   Ad puteum multum flentes.

For his love that you der boght,
Hold you stil and jangel noght,
   Sed prece deponentes 15

The blis of heven than may ye wyn—
God bryng us al to his in,
   Amen! amen! dicentes.

79

(a)

N.L.S., MS. Advocates 18.7.21, f. 85ʳ

Lord Jesu, thin ore!
I sorwe and sike sore;
   That bringet me to grunde.
I have senned sore,
With sennes lesse and more; 5
   Allas! allas, the stounde!

(b)

New College, Oxford, MS. 88, f. 181ᵛ

Louerd, thou clepedest me,
An ich nagt ne ansuarede the

No. 78. 12 *multum] deciphered by Sisam*   13, 14 boght, noght] *MS.* boghth,
nogth   17 us] *added above the line*

Bute wordes scloe and sclepie:
'Thole yet! Thole a litel!'
Bute 'yiet' and 'yiet' was endelis,   5
And 'thole a litel' a long wey is.

80

Balliol College, Oxford, MS. 354, f. 155ᵛ

In noontyde of a somers day,
   The sunne shon full meryly that tyde,
I toke my hawke, me for to play,
   My spanyellis renyng by my syde.
A fesaunt henne than gan I see;   5
   My houndis put her to flight.
I lett my hawke unto her fle,
   To me yt was a deynte syght.

My fawkon flewe fast unto her pray,
   My hownd gan renne with glad chere,   10
And sone I spurnyd in my way—
   My lege was hent all wyth a breer.
This breer, forsothe, yt dyde me gref;
   Ywys yt made me to turne aye,
For he bare wrytyng in every leff—   15
   This Latyn word, *revertere*.

I hayld and pullid this breer me fro,
   And rede this word full enterly,
My hart fell down unto my to,
   That was before full lykyngly.   20
I lett my hauke and fesaunt fare;
   My spanyell fell down unto my kne—
It toke me with a sighyng sare,
   This new lessun: *revertere*.

No. 79. 4, 5 yet, yiet] *MS.* þet, þiet
  No. 80. 1 in noontyde] *MS.* in a tyme *L.* noontijd *T.* in a noone hete
5 than] *L.*, *T.* soone   12 all wyth] *T.* *MS.* in   18 enterly] *MS.* meryly
L. hendeli *T.* enteryly.

Lykyng ys moder of synnes all,   25
    And norse to every wykyd dede,
To myche myschef she makyth men fall,
    And of sorow the dawnce she doth lede.
This hawke of yowth ys high of porte,
    And wildnes makyth hym wyde to fle,   30
And ofte to fall in wykyd sorte,
    And than ys best *revertere*.

THE FRAIL LIFE OF MAN
THE LAST THINGS

81

B.M., MS. Harley 2316, f. 25ʳ

Kyndeli is now mi coming
Into this world with teres and cry;
Litel and pouere is myn having,
Britel and sone ifalle from hi;
Scharp and strong is mi deying,   5
I ne wot whider schal I;
Fowl and stinkande is mi roting—
On me, Jesu, thow have mercy!

82

B.M., MS. Harley 913, f. 32ʳ

Lollai, lollai, litil child, whi wepistou so sore?
Nedis mostou wepe; hit was iyarkid the yore
Ever to lib in sorow, and sich and mourne evermore,
As thin eldren did er this, whil hi alives wore.
    Lollai, litil child, child lolai, lullow,   5
    Into uncuth world icommen so ertow!

No. 80. 29 hawke] *T.* herte   31 sorte] *L.*, *T.*   *MS.* thowght
No. 81. 2 this world with] *MS.* ʒis wiht   4 Britel] *MS.* briʒel   6 wot]
MS. woth
No. 82. 3 evermore] (*Sisam*)   *MS.* ever   4 wore] *MS.* were

Bestis and thos foules, the fisses in the flode,
And euch schef alives, imakid of bone and blode,
Whan hi commith to the world hi doth ham silf sum gode—
Al bot the wrech brol that is of Adamis blode.   10
 Lollai, lollai, litil child, to kar ertou bemette,
 Thou nost noght this worldis wild bifor the is isette.

Child, if betidith that thou ssalt thrive and the,
Thench thou wer ifostred up thi moder kne;
Ever hab mund in thi hert of thos thinges thre—   15
Whan thou commist, what thou art, and what ssal com of the.
 Lollai, lollai, litil child, child lollai, lollai,
 With sorow thou com into this world, with sorow ssalt wend
  awai.

Ne tristou to this world, hit is thi ful vo,
The rich he makith pouer, the pore rich also,   20
Hit turneth wo to wel, and ek wel to wo,
Ne trist no man to this world, whil hit turnith so.
 Lollai, lollai, litil child, thi fote is in the whele,
 Thou nost whoder turne to wo other wele.

Child, thou ert a pilgrim in wikidnes iborn,   25
Thou wandrest in this false world, thou loke the biforn.
Deth ssal com with a blast ute of a wel dim horn,
Adamis kin dun to cast, him silf hath ido beforn.
 Lollai, lollai, litil child, so wo the worp Adam,
 In the lond of Paradis throgh wikidnes of Satan.   30

Child, thou nert a pilgrim bot an uncuthe gest,
Thi dawes beth itold, thi jurneis beth ikest;
Whoder thou salt wend North other Est,
Deth the sal betide with bitter bale in brest.
 Lollai, lollai, litil child, this wo Adam the wroght,   35
 Whan he of the appil ete, and Eve hit him betoght.

16 what thou] *MS.* whan thou 23 thi] *MS.* the 25–8 iborn,
biforn, horn, beforn] *MS.* ibor, bifor, horre, befor 29 worp] *MS.* worþ
31, 32 gest, ikest] *MS.* gist, icast 36 betoght] *MS.* betacht

83

B.M., MS. Add. 22283, f. 130ᵛ

I wolde witen of sum wis wiht
  Witerly what this world were:
Hit fareth as a foules fliht,
  Now is hit henne, now is hit here,
Ne be we never so muche of myht,   5
  Now be we on benche, now be we on bere;
And be we never so war a wiht,
  Now be we seke, now be we fere;
  Now is on proud withoute pere,
    Now is the selve set not by;   10
  And whoso wol alle thing hertly here,
    This worlde fareth as a fantasy.

The sonnes cours, we may wel kenne,
  Ariseth est and goth doun west;
The ryvers into the see thei renne,   15
  And hit is never the more almest.
Wyndes rosscheth here and henne,
  In snouw and reyn is non arest;
Whon this wol stint, ho wot, and whenne,
  But only God on grounde grest?   20
  The eorthe in on is ever prest,
    Nou bidropped, now al druye—
  But uche gome glit forth as a gest,
    This world fareth as a fantasye.

Kunredes come, and kunredes gon,   25
  As joyneth generacions;
But alle heo passeth everichon,
  For alle heor preparacions;

1 wolde] *MS.* wolde wolde   2. Witerly] *MS.* ? wuterly ? witterly   19 and whenne] *Vernon MS.* or

85

Summe are foryete clene as bon
    Among alle maner nacions;   30
So schul men thenken us nothing on
    That nou han the occupacions;
    And alle theos disputacions
        Ideliche alle us occupye,
    For Crist maketh the creacions,   35
        And this world fareth as a fantasie.

Whuch is mon who wot, and what,
    Whether that he be ought or nought?
Of eorthe and eyr groweth up a gnat,
    And so doth mon, whon al is souht;   40
Thaugh mon be waxen gret and fat,
    Mon melteth away so doth a mouht.
Monnes myht nis worth a mat,
    But nuyyeth hym self and turneth to nouht.
    Who wot, save he that al hath wrouht,   45
        Wher mon bicometh whon he schal dye?
    Who knoweth bi dede ought but bi thought?
        For this world fareth as a fantasye.

Dieth mon, and beestes dye,
    And al is on occasion,   50
And al o deth bos bothe drie,
    And han on incarnacion;
Save that men beoth more slyye,
    Al is o comparison.
Ho wot yif monnes soule styye,   55
    And beestes soules synketh doun?
    Who knoweth beestes entencioun,
        On heore creatour how thei crie,
    Save only God, that knoweth heore soun?
        For this world fareth as a fantasye.   60

51 bos] *MSS.* hos   53 slyye] *MS* sley3e   55 wot] *MS.* whot
57 *MS.* who *corrected from* whon

Uche secte hopeth to be save,
    Baldeth bi heore bileeve;
And uchon uppon God thei crave—
    Whi schuld God with hem hym greve?
Uchon trouweth that other rave,   65
    But alle heo cheoseth God for cheve,
And hope in God uchon thei have,
    And bi heore wit heore worching preve.
    Thus mony maters men don meve,
        Sechen heore wittes how and whi,   70
    But Godus merci us al biheve,
        For this world fareth as a fantasye.

For thus men stumble and sere heore witte,
    And meveth maters mony and fele;
Summe leeveth on hym, summe leveth on hit,   75
    As children leorneth forto spele.
But non seoth non that abit,
    Whon stilly deth wol on hym stele.
For he that hext in hevene sit,
    He is the helpe and hope of hele;   80
    For wo is ende of wordes wele—
        Uche lyf loke wher that I lye—
    This world is fals, fikel, and frele,
        And fareth but as a fantasye.

Wharto wilne we forto knowe   85
    The poyntes of Godes privete?
More then hym lust us forto schowe
    We schulde not knowe in no degre;
An idel bost is forto blowe
    A maister of divinite.   90
Thenke we lyve in eorthe here lowe,
    And God an heigh in mageste;

62 Baldeth] V. baldely   68 wit] MS. w^t 87 hym] MS. hy

Of material mortualite
  Medle we, and of no more maistrie.
The more we trace the Trinite,   95
  The more we falle in fantasye.

But leve we ure disputisoun,
  And leeve on hym that al hath wrouht;
We mowe not preve bi no resoun
  How he was born that alle us bouht;   100
But hol in ure entencioun,
  Worschupe we hym in hert and thouht,
For he may turne kuyndes upsodoun,
  That alle kuyndes made of nouht.
    Whon alle ur bokes ben forth brouht,   105
      And al ur craft of clergye,
    And al ure wittes ben thorw-out souht,
      Yit we fareth as fantasye.

Of fantasie is al ur fare,
  Olde and yonge and alle ifere;   110
But make we murie and sle care,
  And worschupe we God whil we ben here;
Spende ur good, and luytel spare,
  And uche mon cheres other cheere.
Thenke hou we come hider al bare—   115
    Ur wey wendyng is in a were—
    Prey we the prince that hath no pere
      Tac us hol to his merci,
    And kepe ur concience clere,
      For this world is but fantasye.   120

Bi ensaumple men may se,
  A gret treo grouweth out of the grounde;
Nothing abated the eorthe wol be
  Thaugh hit be huge, gret, and rounde.

114 other] V. opures

88

Riht ther wol rooten the selve tre,   125
    Whon elde hath maade his kuynde aswounde;
Thaugh ther were rote suche thre,
    The eorthe wol not encrece a pounde.
    Thus waxeth and wanieth mon, hors, and hounde;
        From nought to nought thus henne we hiye,   130
    And here we stunteth but a stounde,
        For this world is but fantasye.

84

Trinity College, Cambridge, MS. 323, f. 47ᵛ

Wen the turuf is thi tuur,
And thi put is thi bour,
Thi wel and thi wite throte
Ssulen wormes to note—
Wat helpit the thenne   5
Al the worilde wnne?

85

Bodl., MS. Laud misc. 23, f. 112ᵛ

Whi is the word belovyd that fals is and veyn?
Sithyn that hise welthis ben uncertayn.

Al so sone slidith his power away
As dooth a brokel pot, that fressh is and gay.

Truste rather to lettris wretyn in th'is   5
Than to this wrecchide world, that ful of synne is.

It is fals in his beheest, and ryght disseyvable;
It hath begiled many a man, it is so unstable.

No. 83. 126 kuynde aswounde] MS. kuyde aswonde   129 wanieth] MSS.
wanteth
    No. 85. 4 brokel] MS. broke   cf., e.g., MS. Trin. Camb. 181 brokil

It is rather to beleve the waverynge wynd
Than the chaungeable world that maketh men so blynd.   10

Whethir thow slepe or wake thow shalt fynde it fals,
Bothe in his besines and in his lustes als.

Telle me, wher is Salamon, that sumtyme was a kyng ryche?
Or Sampson in his strengthe to whom was no man liche?

Or the fair man Absalon, merveylous of cher,   15
Or the duke Jonathas, a wel bylovyd fer?

Wher is bicome Cesar, that lord was of al,
Or the riche man clothid in purpil and in pal?

Telle me wher is Tullius, in eloquens so suete?
Or Arystotil the philosofre wyth hise wittis so grete?   20

Wher been these worthi men that weren here byforn?
Bothe kynges and bisshopis, her power is lorn.

Alle these princes grete wyth her power so hye
Been vanysshid awey with twynklyng of an eye.

The joye of this wrechid world is a short feste—   25
It is likenyd to a shadewe that may not longe leste.

And yit it drawith man fro hevene riche blis,
And ofte tyme makith hym to synne and do amys.

Calle no thing thyn owne therfor, that thow maist her lese;
That the lord hath lent the, eft he wole it cese.   30

Sette thyn herte in heven above, and thynke what joye is there,
And thus to dispise the world I rede that thow lere.

Thow that art wormys mete, powder, and dust,
To enhawnce thiself in pride sette not thi lust

For thow wost not today that thow shalt leve tomorwe: 35
Wherfor do thow evere wel, and thanne shalt thow not sorwe.

9 the waverynge wynd] *other MSS.* the wageryng wynde, the wageryng of
the wynde   30 eft] *MS.* left

It wer ful joyful and swete lordshipe to have
Yif that lordshipe myght a man fro deth save;

But for als moche as a man shal dye at the laste
It is no worshipe, but a charge lordshipe to taaste.   40

86

(a)

B.M., MS. Harley 2253, f. 57ᵛ

> Erthe toc of erthe erthe wyth woh,
> Erthe other erthe to the erthe droh,
> Erthe leyde erthe in erthene throh,
> Tho hevede erthe of erthe erthe ynoh.

(b)

B.M., MS. Egerton 1995, f. 55ʳ

Erthe owte of the erthe ys wounderly wrought,
Erthe of the erthe hath gete a dignyte of nought
Erthe uppon erthe hathe sette alle hys thought
How erthe uppon erthe may be hy brought.

Erthe uppon erthe wolde be a kynge;   5
Howe erthe shall unto erthe thynkythe he noo thynge.
Whenne erthe byddys erthe hys rentes home brynge,
Thenne shalle erthe of the erthe have a pytyus partynge.

Erthe apon erthe wynnys castellis and towrys:
Thenne erthe saythe unto erthe: 'Thys ys alle owrys'.   10
Whenne erthe apon erthe hathe bylde uppe hys bourys,
Thenne shalle erthe for the erthe suffer sharpe schowrys.

No. 85. 38 lordshipe] MS. lorsthipe
No. 86. 2 supplied from Laud Misc. 23   MS. om.   3 alle] most MSS.   MS. om.
10 unto] MS. unt

Erthe goythe apon erthe as molde apon molde;
Erthe gothe apon erthe alle gleterynge in golde,
Lyke as erthe unto erthe nevyr go scholde,   15
And yet shalle erthe unto erthe rathyr thenne he wolde.

Why erthe lovythe erthe woundyr I thynke,
Or why erthe for the erthe swete wylle or swynke,
For whenne erthe apon erthe ys brought withyn brynke,
Thenne shalle erthe of erthe have a foule stynke.   20

Loo, erthe apon erthe, consyder thou may
Howe erthe comythe to erthe nakyd alle way.
Why scholde erthe apon erthe goo stowte and gay,
Syn erthe unto erthe shalle pas in pore aray?

I consylle erthe apon erthe that wyckydly hathe wrought,   25
Whyle erthe ys apon erthe to turne uppe hys thought,
And pray to God apon erthe that alle the erthe hathe wrought,
That erthe owte of the erthe to blys may be brought.

87

B.M., MS. Harley 7322, f. 169^v

Wonne thin eren dinet, and thi nese scharpet,
And thin hew dunnet, and thi sennewess starket,
And thin eyen synket, and thi tunge foldet,
And thin onde stinket, and thin fet coldet,
And thin lippes blaket, and thin teth ratilet   5
And thin honde quaket, and thi throte rutelet,
—Al to late! al to late! Then is te wayn atte yate;
For may thor no man thenne penaunce make.

No. 86. 14 in] *some MSS* as   15 go] *most MSS.   MS. om.*   22 way]
MS. day   *most MSS. which have this stanza read* way.
  No. 87. 4, 6 coldet, rutelet] *MS.* coldetȝ, ruteletȝ

88

B.M., MS. Cotton Faustina B. VI, Part II, f. 1ᵛ

I weende to dede, a kynge iwisse;
What helpis honor, or werldis blysse?
Dede is to mane the kynde wai—
I wende to be clade in clay.

I wende to dede, knight stithe in stoure,   5
Thurghe fyght in felde I wane the flour;
Na fightes me taght the dede to quell—
I wende to dede, soth I yow tell.

I wende to dede, clerk full of skill,
That couth with worde men mare and dill.   10
Sone has me made the dede an ende—
Beese ware with me, to dede I wende.

89

Trinity College, Cambridge, MS. 1157, f. 67ʳ

Farewell, this world! I take my leve for evere;
I am arested to apere at Goddes face.
O myghtyfull God, thou knowest that I had levere
Than all this world to have oone houre space
To make asythe for all my grete trespace.   5
My hert, alas, is brokyne for that sorowe—
Som be this day that shall not be tomorow!

This lyfe, I see, is but a cheyre feyre;
All thyngis passene and so most I algate.
Today I sat full ryall in a cheyere,   10
Tyll sotell deth knokyd at my gate,
And onavysed he seyd to me, 'Chek-mate!'
Lo, how sotell he maketh a devors!
And, wormys to fede, he hath here leyd my cors.

No. 88. 5 to dede] from MS. Add. 37049   MS. om.
No. 89. 7 supplied from MS. Balliol 354

Speke softe, ye folk, for I am leyd aslepe!　　　　15
　　I have my dreme—in trust is moche treson.
Fram dethes hold feyne wold I make a lepe,
　　　But my wysdom is turnyd into feble resoun:
　　　I see this worldis joye lastith but a season—
Wold to God I had remembyrd me beforne!　　　20
I sey no more, but be ware of ane horne!

This febyll world, so fals and so unstable,
　　Promoteth his lovers for a lytell while,
But at the last he yeveth hem a bable
　　　When his peynted trowth is torned into gile.　　25
　　　Experyence cawsith me the trowth to compile,
Thynkyng this, to late, alas, that I began,
For foly and hope disseyveth many a man.

Farewell, my frendis! the tide abidith no man:
　　I moste departe hens, and so shall ye.　　　30
But in this passage, the beste song that I can
　　　Is *Requiem eternam*—I pray God grant it me!
　　　Whan I have endid all myn adversite,
Graunte me in Paradise to have a mancyon,
That shede his blode for my redempcion.　　　35

90

C.U.L., MS. Ee. 1.12, f. 72ᵛ

　　O dredeful deth, come, make an ende!
　　　Come unto me and do thy cure!
　　Thy payne no tunge can comprehende,
　　　That I fele, wooful creature.
　　　O lorde, how longe shall it endure?　　　5
　　Whenne shall I goo this worlde fro,
　　Out of this bitter payne and woo?

No. 89. 19 *supplied from B*　　　25 trowth ... gile] *supplied from B*　　29-35 *supplied from B*

94

Full harde it is for to departe,
   And harde it is this payne to abyde.
O good lorde that in heven art,   10
   Thou be my helpe, comfort, and guyde,
   Both nyght and day and every tyde,
And take my soule into thy blis,
Wherof the joye shall nevir mys.

THE PILGRIM'S FINAL REST

91

B.M., MS. Royal 9. C. II, f. 119ᵛ

Nowe cometh al ye that ben ybrought
   In bondes, full of bitter besynesse
Of erthly luste, abydynge in your thought.
   Here ys the reste of all your besynesse,
   Here ys the porte of peese and resstfullnes   5
To them that stondeth in stormes of dysese,
   Only refuge to wreches in dystrese,
And al comforte of myschefe and mysese.

92

University College, Oxford, MS. 181, f. 42ʳ

Al worship, wisdam, welthe, and worthinesse,
   Al bounte, beaute, joye, and blisfulhede,
Al honoure, vertu, and all myghtynesse,
   Al grace and thankyng unto thi godhede,
   From whom al grace and mercy doth procede!   5
Ay preised be thou, lord in trynyte,
And evere honoured be thi mageste,

No. 91. 1 Nowe] *MS.* Howe   6 dysese] *MS.* dysse (?)   8 mysese]
MS. mysse
   No. 92. 1 wisdam] *MS. Egerton 615   MS.* wellyng

That by mankynde oure noumbre is encresid
   Of thise that longe have ben in pilgrimage,
And now is al hir noyous labour ceesid,   10
   That was bygonne hire firste dayes age;
   Here is the port of siker aryvage.
Honoured be thou, worthi lord on hye!
And welcome be ye to oure compenye!

Now passed bene youre perilous aventures,   15
   And all youre travaile hath an ende take.
Right welcome be ye, blessid creatures!
   Tyme is that scrippe and burdoun ye forsake,
   For now ye schul no lenger journey make;
And after labour time is of quiete,   20
All hevynesse and angwisshe to foryete

For ye have done a noble victory,
   And al youre labour nobely dispendid,
That so ayenst youre troubil enemy
   Youre silven have myghtily defendid;   25
   And that ye have mysdon, it is amendid
By sufferaunce of purgatorie peyne—
Ithanked be thou, Jesu sovereyne!

In heven blis here shole ye be with us
   Unto the day of final jugement,   30
The whiche day ye schul abyde thus
   And preyse God with al youre hole entent,
   While that youre bodi by assignement
Of God is turned to corrupcioun,
And fully shal have his purgacioun.   35

For resoun wole, and also Goddes lawe,
   That he whiche hath done al his besynesse
Fro Goddis will youre lustes to withdrawe,
   Encombrynge you with myche unthriftynesse,

That fro that foule and woful wrecchidnesse   **40**
Hit purged be, and al renewed clene
That manere wey—youre flesche is that we mene—

So at the laste day thei shullen aryse,
  And come byfore the juge sovereyne,
To you conjoyned in a wonder wise,   **45**
  In good accord withouten any peyne
  And in this joye eternally remeyne:
What joy is here ye schul assaye and see—
Honoured be the hye mageste!

42 we] *Bodl. 770, Caxton MS.* I   46 withouten] *Felton MS., Caxton MS.* withoute   47 in] *Bodl. 770 and others MS. om.*   48 ye schul] *Eg., and others MS.* thou shalt

NOTES

1

Index 114. Two tags from a Latin treatise in a 15th-c. MS. The traditional idea that Christ is the 'second Adam' is based upon such New Testament verses as 1 Cor. 15: 22, 45, and Rom. 5: 14 ff. Legend connected the fatal tree of Eden with the wood of the cross (cf. Esther C. Quinn, *The Quest of Seth for the Oil of Life* (Chicago, 1962)). Adam's skull or skeleton is sometimes represented at the foot of the cross (cf. O. Schmitt, *Reallexikon zur deutschen Kunstgeschichte*, i, s.v. 'Adam-Christus', L. Réau, *Iconographie de l'art chrétien*, II, ii (Paris, 1957), pp. 488–91). The idea is used by Donne in his *Hymne to God my God, in my sicknesse:*

> We thinke that *Paradise* and *Calvarie*,
>   *Christs* crosse and *Adams* tree, stood in one place;
> Looke Lord, and finde both *Adams* met in me;
>   As the first *Adams* sweat surrounds my face,
>   May the last *Adams* blood my soule embrace.

2

Index 117. MS. Sloane 2593 (*c.* 1450) is a major collection of English songs and carols. Besides a number of pieces in this selection, it contains such poems as 'I have a gentil cok', 'I have a yong suster', 'Seynte Stevene was a clerk'. The entire MS. was printed by Thomas Wright (*Songs and Carols*) for the Warton Club in 1856, and many of the pieces are to be found in anthologies. For a detailed description of the contents see *EEC*, p. 330, and B. Fehr, *Archiv*, cix (1902), 33–41.

2. *Fowre thowsand wynter*: a traditional estimate. In *Paradiso* xxvi Adam tells Dante that he spent 4,302 years in Limbo; in the York play of the *Harrowing of Hell* (ll. 39–40) he says that he has been there for 4,600 years. According to F. Vigouroux, *Dictionnaire de la Bible*, s.v. 'Chronologie Biblique', there are some two hundred early attempts to date the creation of Adam from the chronological indications in the Hebrew and Septuagint versions of the Old Testament. Cf. also C. A. Patrides, 'Renaissance Estimates of the Year of Creation', *HLQ* xxvi (1963), 315–22.

3. Cf. *EEC*, No. 68:

> Adam our fader was in blis
> And for an appil of lytil prys
> He loste the blysse of Paradys
> Pro sua superbia.

5–8. A lively statement of the paradox known as *felix culpa* from the words of the *Exultet* sung in the Easter Saturday liturgy: 'O certe necessarium Adae peccatum, quod Christi morte deletum est! O felix culpa, quae talem ac tantum meruit habere redemptorem!' For the development of the paradox see A. O. Lovejoy, 'Milton and the Paradox of the Fortunate Fall', *ELH* iv (1937), 161–79: 'The Fall could never be sufficiently condemned and lamented; and likewise when all its consequences were considered, it could never be sufficiently rejoiced over.' The idea is behind the lines in *Paradiso* xxxii (121–3) where Adam is described sitting on the left side of the Queen of Heaven:

> colui che da sinistra le s'aggiusta
> è il padre per lo cui ardito gusto
> l'umana specie tanto amaro gusta

('he that is beside her on the left is the father for whose rash tasting the human kind tastes such bitterness' (tr. Sinclair)). For other examples in ME see *PPl.* (B) V. 488 ff., *CB XIV*, No. 112, 121–4. Cf. also Woolf, pp. 290–1.

3

Index 1244. MS. 15th c. This is the 'song of Adam and Eve' from the *Pilgrimage of the Soul*, a version of the *Pèlerinage de l'âme*, the second part of Guillaume de Guilleville's 14th-century trilogy (on which see Rosemond Tuve, *Allegorical Imagery* (Princeton, 1966), pp. 145–218, and C. S. Lewis, *The Allegory of Love* (Oxford, 1936), pp. 264–71). The English version was obviously a popular work: the *Index* lists eleven MSS. (some of which have illustrations) as well as Caxton's print of 1483. The Felton MS., now in the Melbourne Public Library (C.U.L. has a microfilm) has some additional matter in the songs. This song occurs towards the end of the work (it corresponds to ll. 10,616 ff. of the French poem). The pilgrim is granted a vision of Paradise, in which he sees a 'wonder hye tree that bare grete plentee of fruyt and also of leves'. At its foot stand a multitude of people, making 'an huge feeste of grete solempnite'. His angel explains that these are his 'olde parentes Adam and Eve and stondynge aboute hem myche of her lynage'. The fair tree is that on which grew the apple 'by whiche the cursed Sathanas had deceyued Adam and Eve'. Adam looks up at a dry branch crossed by another branch, and thanks the sovereign Lord for his redemption 'that was made thereby what tyme that Jesu Crist was honged there upon' (cf. No. 1, note). Angels and St. Peter come down with food:

'Comith hyder,' seith Seint Petur to Adam and Eve, 'assaieth of a litel mete whiche that I have broght you, and provith yif it be bettir than the appill whiche that ye have ete, and whethir is more delicious the olde fruyt or the newe. . . .' Than come Adam forth and his wyf Eve and the covent with hem and receyvven of this mete with grete devocioun, and after seiden graces wonder joyfully, takynge eche other by the honde, and Adam bygynneth and alle these othre answeryn sewyngly as ye schul here herafter, for this is the sentence of her seieng.

25. *Fyve thousand yere*: cf. No. 2, l. 2 note.

4

The yates of Parais: *Index* 3357. The verse appears in the midst of a number of moral and mnemonic tags. In the MS. (see No. 14 note) it is followed by the remark *Ideo ista humilitas dici potest 'clavis David', de quo habetur Apocalypsi 3. que claudit, & nemo aperuit* (the reference is to Apoc. 3: 7, with the *clavis David* of Isa. 22: 22 taken to refer to the Virgin Mary). Traditionally, Mary is the 'second Eve', who by her humble obedience to the will of God allowed the damage of the Fall to be repaired. Cf. *Paradiso* xxxii, 4–6:

> La piaga che Maria richiuse e unse
> quella ch'è tanto bella da' suoi piedi
> è colui che l'aperse e che la punse

('the wound that Mary closed and anointed, she at her feet (Eve) who is so fair it was that opened it and pierced it' (Sinclair)). See also Woolf, pp. 115–16.

Heil, Marie, ful of wynne: *Index* 1064. (MS. 14th c.). The tag occurs immediately after a version of the Pater Noster. Gabriel's words to Mary were of significance and potency (cf. the story of the knight who was saved by learning 'two words' (Tryon, *PMLA* xxxviii (1923), 319–20, 374–86)). There are a number of ME versifications of the

Angelic Salutation, some of which were no doubt used as private prayers, and the words were used as the basis of longer poems of adoration to the Virgin.

5

Index 707. C.U.L., MS. Add. 5943 (formerly the property of Lord Howard de Walden) is a 15th-century collection of carols, songs, religious tracts and sermons, and miscellaneous memoranda (see *EEC*, p. 341). There is a longer version of this poem in N.L.S., MS. Advocates 19.3.1.

1. '*Ecce, ancilla Domini!*': Luke 1: 38.

3. *gracyously*. The scene is often treated in a romantic or chivalric manner. Cf. the legend that 'courtesy' came down from heaven when Gabriel addressed Mary (*The Lytylle Childrenes Lytil Boke*, ed. Furnivall, EETS xxxii, p. 16), and *Paradiso* xxxii, 103 ff.:

> qual è quell'angel che con tanto gioco
> guarda nelli occhi la nostra regina,
> innamorato sì che par di foco? . . .
> . . . Baldezza e leggiadria
> quant'esser puote in angelo ed in alma,
> tutta è in lui . . .

('who is that angel that gazes with such rapture on the eyes of our queen, so enamoured that he seems on fire?' . . . 'All confidence and gallant bearing are in him' (Sinclair)). In paintings of the Annunciation, Gabriel sometimes kneels before the Virgin (cf. Simone Martini's *Annunciation* in the Uffizi), and is often represented as a young and handsome man. The idea is turned to comic effect in a much more earthy context in Boccaccio's story of Frate Alberto (*Decameron*, Day IV, 2):

> My Lady Vanity then said that she was highly flattered to be beloved of the Angel Gabriel. . . and that he was welcome to visit her as often as he liked . . . on the understanding, however, that he should not desert her for the Virgin Mary whom she had heard he did mightily affect, and indeed 'twould so appear, for, wherever she saw him, he was always on his knees at her feet (tr. Hutton).

5. *spyce* is sometime figuratively applied to persons. Cf. *Pearl* 235: 'Ho profered me speche, þat special spece.'

21. *hys tabernacle*: a traditional figure of the Virgin, derived from the tabernacle of Moses, containing the Ark of the Covenant. Cf. also Ps. 18

(Vg.): 6: 'In sole posuit tabernaculum suum', which is echoed in some hymns, e.g.

> Ave, de cujus intimo
> Christus processit thalamo
> In sole tabernaculum
> Fixit, qui regit saeculum (Mone, ii, p. 234).

Cf. Lydgate, *A Balade in Commendation of Our Lady* (ed. J. Norton-Smith, John Lydgate. *Poems* (Oxford, 1966), l. 140 and note).

6

Index 1367. On MS. see No. 2 note. This lyric has been set to music by Benjamin Britten and others, and has been the subject of much critical discussion (notably by Davies, pp. 14–19, Woolf, p. 287, and Barbara Raw, *MLR* lv (1960), 411–14). It has been suggested that it is based on an earlier lyric 'Nu this fules singet and maketh hure blisse' (*CB XIII*, No. 31).

1. *mayden*. MS. *mydē* seems likely to be a scribal error (cf. the spelling *maydyn* in l. 9, and elsewhere in the MS.). Perhaps the extra-metrical *A* after *syng* was in some way the source of the error.

7

Index 2645. MS. Egerton 613 contains works of the 13th–15th centuries. The English pieces include the *Poema Morale* and a few religious lyrics. This poem is also found in Trinity College, Cambridge, MS. 323 (13th c.; see No. 8 (b) note) The poet does not always seem to have been able to maintain his rhyme-scheme, and the scribes of both MSS. were rather careless. In a later MS., of the 15th century, Bodl. Ashmole 1393, there is a rearranged version of the poem with a burden, an interesting example both of 'the process of turning an already existing poem in another form into a carol' (*EEC*, p. 392) and of the way in which some early lyrics seem to have retained their popularity (cf. No. 6 note).

1. *Of on*: cf. Trinity MS. *For ou* (Ashmole *A lady . . . brought forth*). The opening ll. in Eg. and T. are probably best regarded as an example of a mixed construction. An invocation with *O!* would make simpler sense, but *O on* is most unlikely. Possibly behind the immediate antecedent of Eg. and T. lay a version with the reading *O þou*; *is* would then be a Northern 2 sg. (another possible example occurs in l. 17) and might have been a source of error to a Southern copyist.

2. *maris stella*: a traditional image of the Virgin Mary. The best-known example is in the hymn *Ave Maris Stella* (found first in the 9th century), of which there are several ME versions. *Maris stella* was sometimes supposed to be the meaning of the name Maria.

11. *Rosa sine spina*: a traditional version of the image of the Virgin Mary as a rose (cf. Ecclus. 24: 18: 'quasi palma exaltata sum in Cades, et quasi plantatio rosae in Jericho'). Cf. Mone, ii, No. 524:

> Salve verbi sacra parens,
> flos de spina spina carens,
> flos spineti gloria;
>
> Nos spinetum, nos peccati
> spina sumus cruentati,
> sed tu spinae nescia . . .

32. *With 'Ave' it went away* . . . The salutation *Ave* reverses the ill-fated name of *Eva*—the Virgin ('blest Mary, second Eve') by her humility repaired the damage wrought by Eve. This is a common idea. Cf. *Ave Maris Stella*:

> Sumens illud Ave
> Gabrielis ore
> Funda nos in pace
> Mutans Evae nomen.

Sometimes there is a pun on *Ave | a vae*. Cf. Mone, ii, No. 496 (an elaboration of the *Ave Maris Stella*):

> Sumens illud ave,
> tanquam procul a vae,
> sic es salutata.

8

To geff pees to men of good wyll: *Index* 3753. MS. 15th c.

Of one stable was his halle: *Index* 2644. The MS. (1255–60), containing material for preachers (probably Franciscans), compiled in the Worcester–Hereford area, is one of the most important collections of eME lyrics (pr., with full discussion, by Reichl). The verse is accompanied by some Latin lines: 'Bernardus clamat: Si rex es, ubi est aula regis, ubi tronus, ubi curie regalis frequencia? aula est stabulum, tronus est presepium, curie regalis frequencia marie presencia.' It is a simple statement of a favourite devotional paradox—the contrast between the sublimity of the Son of

NOTES

God and the humility of the circumstances of his Incarnation (see Erich Auerbach, *Mimesis* (tr. W. R. Trask, Princeton, 1953), ch. 7). Cf. the similar tag in N.L.S., MS. Advocates 18.7.21, f. 119:

He that was al evene with him that al hat wrouht
Als a wreche he hat him lowed, and mad himself as nouht;
A thrallis robe thei han him taken, that lord of miht that hadde no nede;
It semet he hadde himself forsaken to ben clad in mannis wede.

A later example (aptly quoted by Woolf, p. 153) is in Southwell's 'New Prince, New Pompe':

> This stable is a Princes courte,
> The cribb His chaire of State.

9

Index 2733. MS. Arch. Selden B. 26 contains an important collection of songs and carols from the 15th century. On the MS. see Greene, *Sel.*, pp. 176–8. The music of this carol is printed in Sir John Stainer, *Early Bodleian Music* (London, 1901), ii, p. 122. Another text (C.U.L., MS. Ll. 1.11) is pr., with music, in J. Stevens, *Medieval Carols* (*Musica Britannica*, iv, London, 1952). The poem is inspired by a verse from an Advent Epistle (Rom. 13 : 11–12), 'Now it is high time to awake out of sleep; for now is our salvation nearer than when we believed. The night is far spent, the day is at hand.' The two lines at the head of the carol are the refrain or 'burden', which is repeated after each stanza (as in the other carols, Nos. 10–13, 15–16).

4. *bereth the belle*: apparently a familiar phrase denoting excellence, though the exact reference is disputed (cf. Greene, *Sel.*, p. 193). It may be to the bell given as a prize at country races, or to the bell carried by the bell-wether leading the flock.

10

Index 112. MS. Eng. poet. e. 1 (second half 15th c.) is another important collection of songs and carols (see *EEC*, pp. 337–8, Greene, *Sel.*, pp. 179–80). Two stanzas of the carol were used in the Coventry Shearmen and Taylors' Pageant. A MS. (now lost) containing them also had a musical setting (cf. *Renaissance News*, x (1957), 5–7). The shepherds, who play such an attractive part in mystery plays and in the artists' depictions of their scenes with the angels and in adoration at Bethlehem, are always (like their classical predecessors) associated with music. In the Holkham Bible picture book, they

> Songen alle wid one stevene
> Also the angel song that cam fro hevene;

in the Chester play, they all sing—*tunc omnes pastores cum aliis adiuvanti-bus cantabunt hilare carmen.*

11

Index 3460. MS. Balliol 354 (e. 16th c.) is the commonplace book of Richard Hill, a grocer of London, which contains a famous and extensive collection of English poems (see *EEC*, pp. 339–40, R. Dyboski, EETS, ES ci, pp. xiii–lix, R. A. B. Mynors, *Cat. of MSS of Balliol Coll., Oxford* (Oxford, 1963), pp. 352–4). The clarity of the visual detail in this carol suggests a painting (cf., e.g., the Adoration window at East Harling, Norfolk), or a scene from a mystery play (cf. the Towneley *Secunda Pastorum*).

3. *tarbox*: one of the characteristic appurtenances of a shepherd, who used tar as a salve for his sheep.

7. 'The symbolic union between the sound of reed pipes and the crèche in the stable . . . of pastoral music with its characteristic drone and Christmas, pervades more than five hundred years of music up to the *Christmas Oratorio* of Johann Sebastian Bach, and to Handel's *Messiah*, and still further' (E. Winternitz, *Musical Instruments and their Symbolism in Western Art* (London, 1967), p. 132).

20. *Mall . . . Will*: apparently the names of sheep, a favourite ewe and the bell-wether.

29. *Warroke*: obscure, possibly the name of Wat's helper.

53. *cape*: the rhyme suggests 'cap' (rather than 'cape' or 'cope'), 'commonly applied [*OED*] to every kind of male head-dress which is not called a "hat", from which it is distinguished by not having a brim, and by being usually of some soft material' (Wat has a 'hat' and a 'hood'). Cf. the Adoration of the Shepherds in the East window of St. Peter Mancroft, Norwich, where Joseph, sitting warming himself at a brazier, wears a round fur cap.

12

Index 3536. The MS. (*c.* 1425–50) is a roll (now badly worn) containing carols with music; cf. Stevens, *Musica Britannica*, iv, pp. 10 ff. The first

three Latin phrases are from the 12th-century sequence, *Laetabundus /
exsultet fidelis chorus* (*OBMLV*, No. 113).

1. Cf. No. 7, l. 11 note.

13

Index 1351. On MS. Sloane 2593 see No. 2 note.

14

Index 1847. MS. Harley 7322 (l. 14th c.) contains a number of English
religious lyrics interspersed in Latin prose works (see Furnivall, *Political,
Religious and Love Poems*, EETS xv, pp. 249–72 (revised ed.), pp. 220–43
(original ed.). The stanzas also occur in MS. Advocates 18.7.21 (the
preaching-book of John Grimestone; see No. 15 note). In both MSS.
they are preceded by a single stanza which seems to be an appeal of
Christ addressed to Man:

> Leorne to love as ich love the!
> On alle my lymes thou miht se   [*MS*. seo
>   Hou sore ich quake for colde;
> For the ich soffre muche cold and wo.
> Love me wel and no-mo—
>   To the itake and holde.

In the Harley MS. the rubric which follows—'et regina mater sua
nichil habuit unde posset eum induere; ideo dixit sibi'—shows that the
scribe or compiler has taken this stanza to be addressed to the Virgin
Mary. Woolf (pp. 156–7) argues that two distinct poems have become
'associated or joined through the frequency of the dialogue form and the
chance identity of metre'. It is hard to be certain about this, but the two
stanzas here printed make a self-contained and impressive lullaby. The
simple and warm sentiments of the lullaby are given attractive expression
in a number of ME Nativity lyrics and carols (see Woolf, pp. 151–7). In
the Advocates MS. these two stanzas are followed by two more which
entirely lack their homely intensity (*CB XIV*, p. 91).

5. *Oxe and asse*. Cf. No. 11, 40–1. A prophecy by Habakkuk (3 : 2: 'in
medio duorum animalium innotesceris' in the older Latin versions) was
taken to signify that Christ would be born in the presence of an ox and
an ass (see *EEC*, p. 365, and ibid., Nos. 70, 72, and *NQ*, 2nd series (1860),
456).

12–13. The cold weather at the Nativity is often alluded to. Cf. the
York play of the *Journey to Bethlehem*, and the Towneley *Secunda Pastorum*.

Index 2024. MS. Advocates 18. 7. 21 is the preaching-book of John Grimestone, a Franciscan, written 'cum magna solicitudine' in 1372. The MS. is probably from SW. Norfolk. It is a collection of material for sermons, and contains a large number of English verses (cf., besides the pieces printed here, *CB XIV*, Nos. 55–76). On Grimestone and his MS. see *CB XIV*, pp. xvi–xix; a full description is given by Wilson. This carol also appears in MS. Harley 7358. The speaker is not the Virgin Mary, but the poet (and his reader) who imaginatively 'becomes' Eve, the source of mankind's woe.

16

Index 2551.8. The MS. of the Coventry Shearmen and Taylors' Pageant was destroyed by fire in 1879, but the text is preserved in Sharp's ed. of 1825 (see Hardin Craig, *Two Coventry Corpus Christi Plays*, EETS, ES lxxxvii (1957)). The music is pr. in *Oxford Book of Carols*. The carol is to be sung by the women whose children are killed during the Massacre of the Innocents.

7–8. According to a rubric in the play 'here Erode ragis in the pagond and in the strete also'. He is usually made into a blustering tyrant (cf. Hamlet's phrase 'it out-herods herod').

17

Index 158.3. MS. first half 15th c. A little lament, or fragment of a lament, sung by Mary Magdalene, Mary Salome, and Mary the mother of James at the tomb of Christ in the Cornish play of the *Resurrection* (see F. E. Halliday, *The Legend of the Rood* (London, 1955), pp. 13, 112–14, E. Norris, *Ancient Cornish Drama* (Oxford, 1859, 2 vols.) ii, p. 58). It is here used to introduce a number of lyrics on the Passion.

18

Index 94. On MS. see No. 15 note. This poem is a dramatic treatment of Christ's anguish in Gethsemane (cf. Matt. 26: 42, Mark 14: 35).

1–2. The scriptural image of the 'bitter cup' was much used in medieval literature (it was sometime applied, for example, to Eve); see the material collected by G. V. Smithers, *EGS* iv (1951-2), 67-75, and Carleton Brown, *Speculum*, xv (1940), 389-99.

19

Index 2273. C.U.L., MS. Dd. 5.64 (l. 14th c.) contains Rolle's *Ego Dormio*, *The Commandment*, and *The Form of Living*, and a number of lyrics, which are printed by Carleton Brown (*CB XIV*, pp. 93-109) under the heading of 'the School of Rolle'. The question of Rolle's authorship is discussed by Carleton Brown (p. xix), and by Hope Emily Allen (*English Writings of Richard Rolle* (Oxford, 1931), p. 132), who comes to the conclusion that in the case of this poem it is 'possible, though unlikely'. The fifth stanza of the poem is quoted in one text of the *Meditations on the Passion* (Allen, *English Writings*, p. 24). See also Woolf, pp. 163, 382.

6. *prime:* Cf. Kennedy's poem on the Passion (J. A. W. Bennett, *Devotional Pieces in Verse and Prose*, p. 22).

16. A difficult line. It seems to refer to the raising of the cross with the body of Christ already nailed on it. Cf. Nicholas Love's *Mirrour of the Blessed Lyf of Jesu Christ* (ed. L. F. Powell, Oxford, 1908), p. 239: 'and after with all hir myght lifte uppe the crosse with hym hongynge also hye as thay myght and than lete hym falle doun in to the morteys.' Cf. *CB XV*, No. 6, 75-6:

> Thou stone, howe durst thou be so frayll
> To be a mortes wherin his crosse stode?

The cruel jolt of the dropping of the cross into the mortice is sometimes remarked (cf. the lyric pr. *Archiv*, clxvi. 196).

Stab may be a verb (*CB XIV*, gl.) 'thrust', or possibly a noun, a form of *stob/stub* = 'stake, tree stripped of its branches', i.e. the cross. *Stekked* (*CB XIV*, gl. '(?) fixed in position') might = 'pierced' or 'fixed' (cf. *OED*, steek v.²).

21-4. A reference to the favourite image of Christ the Knight. The poem which immediately precedes this in the MS. (No. 45 of this *Selection*) has a similar allusion. Cf. also No. 28, and *CB XIV*, No. 63. The best-known use of this image in ME is in *Piers Plowman* (B XVIII), the earliest the charmingly told exemplum in *Ancrene Wisse* (ed. Tolkien, EETS ccxlix, pp. 198-200, ed. Shepherd (London, 1959), pp. 21-3, 55-8). It is discussed by Woolf, pp. 44-56, and in 'The Theme of Christ the Lover-Knight in medieval English literature', *RES*, n.s. xiii (1962), 1-16, by W. Gaffney, *PMLA* xlvi (1931), 155-68, and Sister Marie de

Lourdes de May, *The Allegory of the Christ-Knight in English Literature* (Washington, 1932).

20

Index 4088. Durham Cathedral, MS. A. III, 12 (containing various theological tracts, sermons, etc.) is dated 1220–40 by S. Harrison Thomson, ('The Date of the Early English Translation of the "Candet Nudatum Pectus"', *MÆ* iv (1935), 100–5), who suggests that it may perhaps have been connected with the school of Robert Grosseteste. The English verses are a translation of a passage in the *Liber Meditationum* of John of Fécamp:

Candet nudatum pectus. Rubet cruentum latus. Tensa arent viscera. Decora languent lumina. Regia pallent ora. Procera rigent brachia. Crura dependent marmorea. Et rigat terebratos pedes beati sanguinis unda.

They were sometimes inserted into longer poems (cf. the lyric in Rolle's *Ego Dormio* (Allen, *English Writings*, p. 68), *CB XIV*, No. 83, ll. 36–40, F. M. Comper, *Spiritual Songs* (London, 1936), p. 133). They seem to have remained popular for a long time: there is a free version in Grimestone's preaching-book. For a full discussion of all the versions, see Woolf, pp. 28–30.

21

Index 2320. MS. c. 1275–1300. This quatrain is found in the extremely popular and influential *Merure de Seinte Eglise* by St. Edmund of Canterbury (d. 1240), a work which exists also in Latin (*Speculum Ecclesiae*) and ME versions. Over sixty MSS. in the three languages are extant. It is a treatise on contemplation, probably intended for religious, and is marked by a vivid affective piety. On it see M. Dominica Legge, *Anglo-Norman Literature and its Background* (Oxford, 1963), pp. 211–12, W. A. Pantin, *The English Church in the Fourteenth Century* (Cambridge, 1955), pp. 222–4, and H. W. Robbins, *Le Merure de Seinte Eglise* (Lewisburg, 1925). The Latin is ed. Helen P. Forshaw, S.H.C.J., *Edmund of Abingdon: Speculum Religiosorum and Speculum Ecclesiae* (Auctores Britannici Medii Aevi, iii, London, 1973). Cf. also her articles in *Archives d'histoire doctrinale et littéraire du Moyen Âge*, 38 (1971), 39 (1972). (The English quatrain is not in the earliest Latin version of the text (*Speculum Religiosorum*), but is found in the later 'vulgate' version (*Speculum Ecclesiae*) which is

translated from one of the Anglo-Norman versions.) The lines occur at
the end of the section 'de contemplacion devaunt midi'; in the Selden
MS. they are introduced thus:

> Ci devez penser de la duce Marie, de quel anguisse ele estoit replenie
> quant ele estut a son degre. . . . 'Ne me apelez pas bele, taunt ne quunt,
> mes amere me apelez des ore en avaunt, par de amertume e de dolour
> graunt me ad ore repleni ly tut pussaunt' . . . cele reson dit ele en le chaunson
> de amor: 'Ne vous amerveylez si ie suy brunecte e haule qar le solail me ad
> tote descolouree.' E pur ceo dit un Engleis en tel manere de pite . . .

Carleton Brown thought it more than likely that St. Edmund composed
the English verses himself, but the attribution to 'un Engleis' suggests
rather that he is making use of an already existing poem (see also Woolf,
p. 242). The 'chaunson de amor' is the Canticum Canticorum (1: 5:
'Nolite me considerare quod fusca sim, quia decoloravit me sol'). The
poem is a fine literary example of the 'manere de pite', compressed and
allusive, yet powerfully suggesting the sorrow and darkness of the scene
at Calvary. The image of the setting sun suggests both the sorrow of the
natural world at the death of its creator, and the death of Christ, the *sol
justitiae*. Cf. *The Dream of the Rood*, ll. 52–6, Abelard:

> Dum crucem sustinens sol verus patitur
> Sol insensibilis illi compatitur
> > (*Hymnarius Paraclitensis*, ed. G. M. Dreves (Paris,
> > 1891), p. 113)

and Donne:

> There I should see a Sunne, by rising set,
> And by that setting endlesse day beget.
> > (*Goodfriday, 1613. Riding Westward*)

1. *Nou:* (?) *conj.* = 'now that' (see C. T. Onions, *MÆ* xvii (1948) 32-3).

22

Index 4159, a lyric from Grimestone's preaching-book (cf. No. 15 note).
See Woolf, pp. 249–50. It is similar to a passage in the *Liber de Passione
Christi* (*PL* clxxxii. 1133–42) in which the Virgin Mary gives her own
account of the Passion, and appeals to the Jews to crucify her with her
son: 'O Judaei, ipsi nolite mihi parcere, qui natum meum crucifixistis.
Matrem crucifigite, aut alia quacunque me saeva morte perimite. Dum
meo cum filio finiar simul, male solus moritur.'

The theme is also found in Latin hymns; cf.

> Nato, quaeso, parcite,
> Matrem crucifigite,
> Aut in crucis stipite
> Nos simul affigite,
> Male solus moritur.
> (Dreves, xx. 199.)

The *planctus Mariae* or 'complaint' of Mary is a type of poem which is popular in the West from the 12th century. Beside the tradition that the Virgin bore the sorrows of her Son's Passion with heroic fortitude ('stantem illam lego, flentem non lego', says St. Ambrose), there developed a natural urge to portray her maternal anguish in a more dramatic and human way. Not only does she weep, but she falls unconscious, or wishes to die herself rather than survive her child. On the *planctus* see Woolf, pp. 246–73, H. Thien, *Über die englischen Marienklagen* (Kiel, 1906), F. J. Tanquerey, *Plaintes de la Vierge en anglo-français* (Paris, 1921). Poems of this type are usually dramatically conceived, either as monologues or as miniature scenes. On the relationship with the medieval drama, see Karl Young, *The Drama of the Medieval Church* (Oxford, 1933), i, pp. 492–539, and G. C. Taylor, 'The English Planctus Mariae', *MP* iv (1906), 605–37.

23

Index 3211. This sequence is found in five other MSS. of the late 13th and early 14th centuries (although in one, MS. Royal 8. F. ii, only the first stanza is given). In this MS. (as in St. John's College, Cambridge, MS. 111) it is accompanied by its music. There is a recording of the sequence on Argo (Z)RG(5)433, 'Medieval English Lyrics', with useful notes by E. J. Dobson and F. Ll. Harrison. The opening of the poem suggests the Latin sequence *Stabat iuxta Christi crucem* (Dreves, viii. 55), of which there are ME renderings (*CB XIII*, Nos. 4, 47). Carleton Brown points out a general source in Latin accounts of the passion in which the Virgin makes her complaint to 'St. Anselm' (*PL* clix. 271 ff.) or to 'St. Bernard' (*PL* clxxxii. 1136). See also Woolf, pp. 245–6.

1–3 A dramatic adaption of John 19: 26–7.

11–12. Cf. Luke 2: 35: 'et tuam ipsius animam pertransibit gladius', which is often recalled in this type of poem (cf. the *Stabat Mater Dolorosa*:

> . . . cuius animam gementem
> contristatam et dolentem
> pertransivit gladius).

24

Index 4189. MS. end 15th c. The poem also appears in Trinity College, Cambridge, MS. 1450 (cf. Rigg, pp. 86–7).

1 ff. The cryptic and dramatic opening is an adaptation of the *chanson d'aventure* (cf. No. 43).

25

Index 2619. MS. 15th c. The poem is found in two other 15th-c. MSS. Cf. Woolf, pp. 256–7. There is also a version of it in the form of a *chanson d'aventure* (*Index* 1447). In this a narrative preface describes how the poet kneeling in church saw a 'pite', the characteristic pietà of late medieval art. Mary, holding the dead Christ in her lap, speaks to him. (On the history of the pietà see Woolf, pp. 392–4.)

26

Ye that pasen be the weyye: *Index* 4263, from Grimestone's preaching-book (see No. 15 note). It is based on Lam. 1: 12: 'O vos omnes qui transitis per viam, attendite et videte si est dolor sicut meus', which was used in Good Friday services. The crucified Christ's dramatic appeal to sinful man became a popular type of religious lyric (see Woolf, pp. 36–44), and four of the longer English examples are given in this section. Comparable shorter poems are *Index* Nos. 110 (*CB XIV*, No. 46), 207, 502. These short dramatic appeals or complaints would obviously be very effective when used in a sermon. There is an example (*Index* 495, Woolf, p. 38) in another influential preacher's manual, the *Fasciculus Morum*. Another (*Index* 1902) is quoted in the *Speculum Sacerdotale* (EETS cc, p. 112). Yet another (*Index* 457) is ingeniously used in a sermon *de Corpore Christi* in C.U.L., MS. Ii. 3.8 (f. 90ʳ):

> Ay bitwene thou lok[e] on me,
> And thenc on hym that yaf the me,
> Hou I am broken for thy sake,
> And nevere ne tac thou other make.

A particularly good example (*Index* 3905.5) appears in a Brussels MS. (Bibl. roy. 2054, f. 48ʳ):

> What ich thole, man, byhald!
> Lyt ic am of the itald.

Wyth al my **myghte** to the ic crie,
On the rode for the ic dye.
Ther nys no pyne ylich myn—
Byhold the sorwe that ic am in!
Byhold the nayles sarpe and kene,
In fet and honden hy be[th] ysene.
More me grevyt unkenden[e]sse of man
Than al the sorwe in wich ich am.

O man unkynde: *Index* 2507 (MS. 15th c.). The poem also occurs in two
other MSS. and in a couple of early printed books. In one MS. (Bodl.,
Tanner 407) the word *hert* is replaced by a drawing of a heart; in the
other (B.M. Add. 37049) it is accompanied by an illustration of the
wounded Christ (the *Imago Pietatis*) indicating a large figure of a heart
(see Woolf, pp. 185-6, Pl. 1). On early devotion to the Sacred Heart
see J. V. Bainvel, *La Dévotion au sacré-cœur de Jésus* (Paris, 1921) (tr. E.
Leahy as *Devotion to the Sacred Heart*, London, 1922). The lines are a sort
of rudimentary emblem poem (see Thomas W. Ross, 'Five Fifteenth-
century "Emblem" Verses', *Speculum*, xxxii (1957), 274–82, Douglas
Gray, 'The Five Wounds of Our Lord', *NQ* ccviii (N.S. 10) (1963),
166–8). The appeal of Christ to man was an obvious form to be used as
a *titulus* to accompany a pious image, or to be displayed publicly to
encourage devotion. Another poem (*CB XV*, No. 108), which seems to
echo these lines in its first stanza, is found as an inscription in Almond-
bury Church, Yorkshire, with the date 1522 (see *Journal of Archaeological
Association*, xxx (1874), 231). Cf. also Lydgate's *Minor Poems*, ed. H. M.
MacCracken, EETS, ES cvii, pp. 250–2.

27

Index 497. MS. Harley 4012 (15th c.) contains various English religious
pieces, including another appeal of Christ from the cross (*CB XV*,
No. 104). At the head of the page on which 'Wofully araide' begins
there is a small drawing of Christ crucified, with blood issuing from his
wounds. In form the poem is a modified carol, with the verses 'through-
set' without a repeated burden (J. Stevens, *Music and Poetry in the Early
Tudor Court* (London, 1961), pp. 370, 372). In the early 16th-century
Fayrfax MS. (B.M.) it is set to music by William Cornish, junior, and
by Browne (see Stevens, pp. 11–12, 103–4, 269–72). It is an interesting
example of a 15th-century lyric which kept its popularity in the follow-
ing century (see Woolf, pp. 206–7). It has sometimes been attributed to

Skelton. It is ascribed to him in one copy in a 16th-century hand on the flyleaf of a printed book (see A. Dyce, *The Poetical Works of John Skelton* (London, 1843), i, pp. 141–3), but such ascriptions are by no means always reliable. A reference in *The Garden of Laurel* seems at first sight more cogent. Skelton here lists among his works 'Wofully arayd and shamefully betrayd'. But in most copies of the poem there is not a hint of the second phrase, and it may be that Skelton's poem was simply using a striking burden from an earlier lyric (see l. 1 note, and cf. Rigg, p. 86). The probability that it is an independent lyric is supported by the rubrics which accompany it in the Harley MS.: 'Hosumever saith this praier in the worship of the passion shal have .c. yere of pardon' and 'Whosumever saith this devotely hathe grauntid be divers bisshopis saing at the laste ende five pater nosters and five Aves .cccccc. dayes of pardon', which suggest a devotional verse prayer unattached to any known author, and perhaps also by the textual variations in the 'Heber' copy (see Dyce, i, p. 141), which has a stanza not found in Harley and a final stanza which is considerably different, and in the fragment in Bodl. MS. Lyell 24, which has a rather different burden:

> Woofully arayde,
> The sonne of a mayd,
> Behold, manne, and se,
> With tresoun betrayed,
> And onne the cros splayd   [*MS. om.* cros
> For the love of the.

The copies of the poem show considerable rhythmical irregularity ('the highly skilled composer John Browne used so corrupt a text for his setting of "Wofully araide" . . . that it cannot be emended without changing the music too drastically' (Frank Ll. Harrison, Notes to Argo record (Z)RG(5)443)); possibly the agreement among the existing MS. copies suggests that this was original.

1. *Wofully araide*: the phrase occurs elsewhere in 15th-century works (see Dyce, ii, p. 197), one at least of which (*The Conuercyon of Swerers*) is an echo of this poem. Cf. the phrase *wrapped in wo* in No. 61, l. 6. Devotional poetry was fond of developing the ironic possibilities of the paradox that Christ in his Passion 'ruled from the cross' and was clad in 'royal garments' (cf. No. 40). There is also a trace here of the ironic use of 'array' to mean 'thrash, beat' (*OED* quotes Caxton's *Reynard*: 'I am so sore arayed, and sore hurte').

26. *so bobbid*: this vigorous word is something of a favourite in descriptions of Christ's Passion. Cf. No. 24 and *CB XV*, No. 10. (Another

example quoted in *OED* comes from a prayer printed in 1578: 'Thou wast . . . buffeted, blindfolded, bobbed with fists.' Professor Bennett points out an even later example in Lancelot Andrewes: 'As they, in the Judgment Hall, worshipped Him with *Ave Rex*, and then gave Him a bobb blind-fold' (Sermon 15 Of the Nativitie: Christmas 1622, in Lancelot Andrewes, *Sermons*, ed. G. M. Story (Oxford, 1967), p. 114). G. R. Owst, *Literature and Pulpit in Medieval England* (revised ed., Oxford, 1961, p. 510) quotes a 15th-century sermon's description of a contemporary game called 'the bobbid game' in which a blindfold victim is struck and has to guess which was his assailant (it survives as 'Hot Cockles'), 'which is that which the soldiers played with Christ at his Passion'. The use of this in the mystery plays is discussed by Kolve, pp. 185–6.

28. *not demed.* F. *not deynyd*, for which Stevens suggests 'not in a haughty spirit (?)'. *not demed* will make sense if we take it as *nought demed*, 'judged, thought to be of no worth'. Alternatively, '[actual], not imagined' (Davies).

28

Index 2150. The verses are written in a hand of the second half of the 14th c. (Carleton Brown). See Woolf, pp. 54–6.

11–18. A simple and bold use of the image of Christ as the Lover-Knight (see No. 19, ll. 21–4 note). Cf. *Towneley Plays* (ed. G. England, EETS, ES lxxi, p. 261), where, in the Crucifixion play, one of the torturers cries:

> Stand nere, felows, and let se
> How we can hors oure kyng so fre!

The passage (ll. 101–18) has the same ironic use of the words *ryde* and *palfray*. See Kolve, p. 193.

17. *Under mi gore.* This poet visualizes his knightly Christ wearing some sort of garment or robe, not the simple loin-cloth which was by this time common in depictions of the Crucifixion.

29

Index 2241. MS. Add. 46919 (formerly Phillipps 8336) contains a series of English verse translations of Latin hymns and liturgical pieces by William Herebert, a Franciscan. The *Lanercost Chronicle* records his presence in Paris in 1290; in 1314 he was at the Oxford convent, and became forty-third lector in Divinity about 1320. He seems to have been a man of some learning: he knew the works of Grosseteste, annotated Roger Bacon, and gave a copy of Bede's *De Temporum Ratione* to the Grey Friars at Hereford (see A. B. Emden, *A Biographical Register of the University of Oxford to A.D. 1500* (Oxford, 1957), ii, pp. 911–12, *CB XIV*, pp. xiii–xiv). Herebert's English poems are printed in *CB XIV*, and (by Helmut Gneuss) in *Anglia*, lxxviii, 169–92. They are generally wooden and pedestrian, but one or two, like this and No. 40, have some literary interest. This poem is a version of the *Improperia* or 'reproaches' sung on Good Friday, in which Christ reminds his people of his kindness and protection under the Old Covenant (and which is finely used by the later poet Herbert in *The Sacrifice*; cf. Rosemond Tuve, *A Reading of George Herbert* (London, 1952)). The lines *popule meus, etc.* are repeated rather like a burden (see Robbins, 'Friar Herebert and the Carol', *Anglia*, lxxv (1957), 196–7). (In this poem, and in others of Herebert's I have left the distinctive *oe* spellings ($=e$) except in rhyming positions.)

30

Index 1699 (MS. *c.* 1400). On the traditional background of this lyric, see the valuable discussion by Woolf, pp. 41–2. Cf. the passage attributed to St. Bernard quoted in the *Golden Legend* (Caxton's version, Temple Classics (London, 1900), i, pp. 72–3):

. . . whereof saith S. Bernard: *Tu es homo*, etc.—He saith thus: Thou art a man and hast a chaplet of flowers, and I am God and have a chaplet of thorns. Thou hast gloves on thine hands, and I have the nails fixed in my hands. Thou dancest in white vestures, and I God am mocked and vilipended, and in the house of Herod had received a white vesture. Thou dancest and playest with thy feet, and I with my feet have laboured in great pain. Thou liftest up thine arms in joy, and I have stretched them in great reproof. Thou stretchest out thine arms across in caroling and gladness, and I stretch mine in the cross in great opprobrium and villainy. Thou hast thy side and thy breast open in sign of vain glory, and I have mine opened with a spear . . .

This poem handles the theme of Christ's 'reproaches' with a much firmer control of irony and paradox than Herebert's slavish version.

11. *Acros thou berest thyn armes*: a reference to ring-dances or 'caroles', in which the participants held hands (see the illustration in Greene, *Sel.*).

18–20. Long, wide slits in clothing were fashionable (see Furnivall, *Hymns to the Virgin and Christ*, EETS xxiv, p. 62, viii–ix). *Spaiers* are openings or slits in gowns (see *OED, spare sb.*²). The word was later restricted to slits in ladies' gowns (in Skelton's *Phyllyp Sparowe*, the sparrow 'was wont to . . . go in at my spayre').

31

MS. 14th c. (this part after 1381; cf. Mynors, *Cat. MSS. Balliol Coll.*, pp. 130–5). The tag is listed in the *Index* as 3433, but it is very similar to *Index* 1977 (*CB XIII*, No. 56). This, in one MS., is accompanied by some Latin lines:

> Memoria passionis tue, o bone Jesu,
> Lacrimas tollit, oculos effundit,
> Faciem humectat, cor dulcorat.

The 'memory' of Christ's Passion is one of the great themes of medieval devotion. Besides the longer examples given here, it is found in a number of shorter tags and verses. Cf. *Index* 1336 (MS. Adv. 18. 7. 21, Wilson, No. 194, p. 40), and *Index* 3239 (MS. Lambeth 78) (see Woolf, p. 39 n. 2):

> Swete Jesu, hwar was thy gylt
>   To suffere so moche wo for me?
> Thy body to harde panys iput,
>   And al todrawe upon a tree,
>
> Feet and hondys inaylyd fast—
>   Jesu, thy paynys weren smert,
> [Th]at yet for me were at the laste
>   Wyth spere istonge to the hert!
>
> Swete Jesu, harde were thy paynys
>   That thow on cros me sufferyst fore;
> That I the have gylt ayens
>   Foryeve me, lord,—I wel no more.

32

Index 1365. MS. Digby 2 (end 13th c.) contains a prognostication of eclipses, various tractates, and devotional verses. The poem also occurs in MS. Harley 2253. It is discussed by Woolf (pp. 65–6), who points out that in it 'the formal echoes of the secular lyric are deftly blended with the tone of elegiac love-longing that colours the whole'.

17. *clungin so the cley*: *cling* = 'shrivel, wither', 'become dispirited'. Cf. *Ludus Coventriae*, ed. K. S. Block, EETS, ES cxx, p. 48, l. 164: 'My herte doth clynge and cleve as clay.'

42. For a legend that the smith was unwilling to do the work, and the nails were made by his wife, cf. R. Morris, *Legends of the Holy Rood*, EETS xlvi, pp. 84–5. Cf. also the *Northern Passion*, ed. Foster, EETS cxlv, ll. 1339–1502.

33

Index 3964. MS. Royal 12. E. 1 (e. 14th c.) contains also the sequence 'Stond wel, moder, under rode' (No. 23). This popular type of poem— a simple expression of devotion and sorrow before the crucified Christ —is discussed by Woolf, pp. 33–4. Cf. *CB XIII*, Nos. 34, 36, 37.

34

Not listed in *Index*. Miss Rosemary Woolf kindly drew my attention to this poem, which occurs in the 15th-century devotional prose work *Dives and Pauper*, in a chapter (xv) on the Passion as a remedy against lechery. She points out that it is a translation of the first three verses of a Latin hymn 'Reminiscens beati sanguinis' (Dreves, viii, No. 11).

35

Index 1787. MS. 15th c. This lyric occurs, written out as prose, in a work on the Passion. The context in which it appears gives special attention to the Precious Blood and the Wounds of Christ, and explains the verse of Isaiah (12: 3) 'hauríetis aquas in gaudio de fontibus salvatoris'— which is often used in this connection—thus: 'Ye schul drawe watres in joye of the welles of oure saveoure, that is to mene: ye schul drawe out witt and wisdom, love and devocioun, pacience and contemplacioun of the woundes of Crist that be welles of oure saveoure.' The idea of Christ's wounds as 'wells' or fountains is common in late medieval religious literature and art. In another 15th-century poem, accompanied by devotional images, in MS. Douce 1, prayers are addressed to each of the wounded limbs in turn, and the 'wells' are named: *well of mercy* (right hand), *welle of grace* (left hand), *welle of lyfe* (heart), *welle of pyte* (right foot), and *welle of comforte* (left foot). In the visual arts the 'Fountain of Life' filled with blood flowing down from the wounds of Christ, and with worshippers kneeling around it, or even climbing in and bathing themselves, is a favourite motif. On this, and on the devotion to the Wounds of Christ, see L. Gougaud, 'Les antécédents de la dévotion au sacré-cœur', *Dévotions et pratiques ascétiques du Moyen Âge* (Paris, 1925), pp. 74–128, D. Gray, 'The Five Wounds of Our Lord', *NQ*, N.S. 10, ccviii (1963), 50–1, 82–9, 127–34, 163–8, and the references there given.

3. *Namely the stronde of hys syde*: the great wound in Christ's side was held in especial veneration. In popular devotion images of the wound, giving what were believed to be its exact measurements, seem to have been regarded as possessing almost magical power.

36

Index 3212. Merton College MS. 248 contains a number of English verses scattered through sermons (see *CB XIV*, Nos. 35–41). The collection was made by John de Shepeye (or Sheppeye) (d. 1360), a Benedictine monk who became prior (1333), then Bishop of Rochester (see A. B. Emden, *A Biographical Register*, iii. 1683). This poem is a translation of a stanza of the hymn by Venantius Fortunatus (*c*. 530–*c*. 600), *Pange lingua gloriosi lauream certaminis*:

> Crux fidelis, inter omnes arbor una nobilis,
> Nulla silva talem profert fronde, flore, germine
> Dulce lignum, dulces clavos, dulce pondus sustinet.

The hymn was sung in Good Friday services. Carleton Brown draws attention to a version (Mone, i, No. 101) in which this stanza is used as a recurrent burden. The cross is 'faithful' because it fulfils its part in the scheme of redemption; it is the cruel instrument of suffering, but also 'sweet' because it is the instrument of salvation (for the paradox cf. 'Allas! the crune of joyye under thornes lay', *CB XIV*, No. 55, 26). There are a couple of instances of the same use in sermon MSS. of stanzas from the hymn *Vexilla Regis prodeunt*. Cf. *Index* 3403 (Merton 248) or 3490.6 (in a sermon of Friar Nicholas Philip):

> The tree of the cros is wol bryghte;
> With kynges porpure it is adyghte.
> Chosyn thou art a worthy tree
> Qwan so holy lemys towchedyn thee.

37

Two tags which are used here to introduce a couple of lyrics on the triumph of Christ in his Passion and Resurrection. The first is a couplet by William Herebert (see No. 29 note). Helmut Gneuss, who prints it in *Anglia*, lxxviii (p. 183), points out that it is a translation of an antiphon which in the Sarum and York use was sung between Easter and Pentecost as a 'memoria de cruce':

> Crucem sanctam subiit
> Qui infernum confregit,
> Accinctus est potentia,
> Surrexit die tertia. Alleluya.

The second is from Merton College MS. 248 (see No. 36 note), and puts in vernacular and mnemonic form a series of Latin lines on the 'comings' of Christ (see *CB XIV*, p. 258). It is followed in the MS. by a similar and equally striking set of verses (Cf. Apoc. 6: 2 ff.):

> He rod upon a whit hors in thet thet he becam man vor the,
> He rod on a red hors in thet thet he was inayled to the rode tre,
> He rod on a blak hors in thet thet he the devel overcam,
> He rod on a dun hors in thet thet the cloude hym up nam . . .

There is a similar lyric in which Christ looks forward to his triumph at the day of Doom (*CB XV*, No. 111):

> I have laborede sore and suffered deyyth,
> And now I rest and draw my breyth;
> But I schall come and call ryght sone
> Hevene and erth and hell to dome;
> And thane schall know both devyll and mane,
> What I was and what I ame.

The figure of the triumphant Christ who has conquered sin and death is not so favoured by the devotional poets as that of the suffering Lord, but the poems which use it often show a remarkable power, in particular, Dunbar's 'Done is a battell on the dragon blak' (William Dunbar, *Poems*, ed. J. Kinsley (Oxford, 1958), No. 3).

38

Index 2684. On MS. see No. 36 note. This is a translation of the first two stanzas of the Easter hymn *Aurora lucis rutilat* (*c.* 6th c.):

> Aurora lucis rutilat,
> Caelum laudibus intonat,
> Mundus exultans iubilat,
> Gemens infernus ululat,
>
> Cum rex ille fortissimus
> Mortis confractis viribus
> Pede conculcans tartaros
> Solvit catena miseros. . . .

(*OBMLV*, p. 49)

39

Index 2528. MS. Arundel 285 (e. 16th c.) probably compiled in pre-Reformation times, is illustrated with woodcuts from printed books. On the MS. and its contents see J. A. W. Bennett, *Devotional Pieces in Verse and Prose* (STS, 3rd ser. xxiii (1949)). The aureate diction sometimes reminds us of Dunbar's poem on the Resurrection.

3. *illumynary*: MS. *illumynar* can mean 'an enlightener' ('lorde God, inspirer and illumynour of prophetes') and 'a source of light, luminary', but the rhyme seems to require *illumynary*. This word is only once attested in the *OED* (in 1692), but seems a possible aureate term.

6. *subtell nycht*: 'thin, not dense' (cf. 'subtle air').

15. *thair strang portes*: cf. Ps. 23 (Vg.): 7, 9: 'attollite portas, principes, vestras, et elevamini portae aeternales, et introibit rex gloriae'. This verse is used dramatically in the Harrowing of Hell plays. It appears in a little dialogue in a sermon (*Index* 3825.5):

> [*Christus*] 'Ondo youre yatys princys to me!
> Helle-yatis oppen ye!
> The kyng of bliss will come in.'
>
> [*demones*] 'Qwat is he that comyn is
> That seyth he is kyng of blys?'
>
> [*Christus*] 'I am lorde of strength and myghte,
> And a stalworthi lord in ich a fyght.'

23. *clym.* Cf. *The Dream of the Rood* 40: 'gestah he on gealgan heanne', Herbert, *The Sacrifice*: 'Man stole the fruit, but I must climbe the tree'. The influential 13th-century *Meditationes Vitae Christi* gives two traditions concerning the method by which Christ was fastened to the cross— one that the cross was laid upon the ground and Christ there nailed upon it (this is followed by the crucifixion plays), and the other, that the cross was in its place erect, and the crucifiers used two ladders for their work, while another shorter ladder was provided in front for Christ. (Cf. the ME version of Nicholas Love, ed. L. F. Powell (Oxford, 1908), pp. 238–9.) This latter version is occasionally found in illustrations of the work (e.g. Corpus Christi College, Oxford, MS. 410, f. 135^v) and in paintings. In one by Guido da Siena (? (*c.* 1270), Christ boldly and dramatically steps on to the cross (see J. White, *Art and Architecture in Italy 1250–1400* (London, 1966), pl. 47 (b)); in another, more serenely conceived, by an assistant of Fra Angelico in San Marco, Florence, Christ stands above his ladder, on the *suppedaneum* (see J. Pope-Hennessy, *Fra Angelico* (London, 1952), Fig. xxvi). Cf. also the ME *Southern Passion* (ed. B. D. Brown, EETS clxix), ll. 1459–61.

27. *lawre croune*: a typically learned reference to the triumph of Christ (early hymns on the cross and passion sometimes use words like *laurea, triumphum, trophaeum*; cf. the *Pange lingua* of Fortunatus).

35. *ordouris nyne.* The angels were traditionally arranged (following the *Celestial Hierarchy* of Dionysius) in three hierarchies of three orders each: Seraphim, Cherubim, and Thrones; Dominations, Virtues, and Powers; Principalities, Archangels, and Angels. Woolf, p. 307, remarks that this stanza 'recalls the *Te Deum* carols' (see *EEC*, Nos. 285–304).

40

Index 3906. By William Herebert (see No. 29 note). The poem is a paraphrase of Isa. 63: 1–7, a description of the Messiah returning in triumph from Edom, which was used as a *lectio* for Wednesday in Holy Week. The Old Testament passage is the basis of a tag in MS. Harley 7322 (*Index* 3907):

> 'Wat is he this that comet so briht
> Wit blodi clothes al bediht?'

respondentes superiores dixerunt:

> 'He is bothe God and man:
> Swilc ne saw [w]e nevere nan.
> For Adamis sinne he suffrede ded
> And therfore is his robe so red.'

Cf. also Lydgate, *Minor Poems*, ed. H. N. MacCracken, EETS, ES cvii, pp. 250–2 (these poems are discussed by Woolf, pp. 199–202); *PPl.* (B) xix, 5 ff.

6. *chaunpyon to helen monkunde in vyht*: cf. Isa. 'Propugnator . . . ad salvandum'. Herebert has drawn out one meaning of *salvare*, and strikingly, if somewhat abruptly, fused the apparently paradoxical figures of Christ as warrior and as physician.

9. *the wrynge*. The image of the treading of a winepress for a crushing disaster or terrible slaughter is found elsewhere in the Old Testament (cf. Lam. 1: 15, Joel 3: 12–13) and is taken into the New (cf. Apoc. 14: 19–20, 19: 15). The commentators take the winepress as a symbol of 'the cross and all its torments', so that the treading of the winepress becomes a deliberately ambiguous image, referring both to Christ's triumph in the Passion and to his suffering (cf. the similar association of pain and 'sweetness' in other crucifixion lyrics). It was also associated with the bunch of grapes (Num. 13: 23) that was brought back to the children of Israel from the Promised Land hung on a staff, which was taken to prefigure the body of Christ, the mystic grape, hung on a cross (cf. St. Augustine: 'primus botrus in torculari pressus est Christus' (*PL* xxxvi. 649), and the depiction in the glass of the east window of Corona at Canterbury (B. Rackham, *The Ancient Glass of Canterbury Cathedral* (London, 1949), p. 75, pl. 28b)). The idea is well used by Lydgate in a poem on the Passion (ed. cit., p. 251):

> In Bosra steyned of purpil al my weede . . .
> The vyne of Soreth railed in lengthe and brede,
> The tendre clustris rent doun in ther rage,
> The ripe grapis ther licour did out shede,
> With bloody dropis bespreynt was my visage . . .

It receives rather grotesque visual expression in the 'Mystic Winepress' of late medieval art, which often depicts the body of Christ crushed beneath a winepress. (On this see E. Mâle, *L'Art religieux de la fin du Moyen Âge en France* (2nd ed., Paris, 1949), pp. 115–22, L. Lindet, 'Les représentations allégoriques du moulin et du pressoir dans l'art chrétien', *Revue archéologique*, xxxvi (1900), 403–13.)

11. Herebert misses the emphatic balanced repetition of the Latin: 'calcavi eos in furore meo et conculcavi eos in ira mea.'

21. *adreynt al wyth shennesse*: Herebert has toned down the bolder Biblical image 'inebriavi eos in indignatione mea.'

22–3. These lines correspond to v. 7 of the Biblical passage. In the MS. they are placed before ll. 20–1 (v. 6). Carleton Brown suggests that the service book which Herebert used omitted verse 6, and that Herebert, noticing the omission, placed it at the end of his translation (the rubric 'istud est de integro libri sed non est de epistola' supports this). It seems best to restore v. 7 = ll. 22–3 to its rightful place, and to interpret it here as a statement by the poet, a personal act of will provoked by the dramatic scene he has presented.

41

Index 143. MS. l. 13th c. The lyric occurs among some Latin notes on the Passion. Another version (listed separately in the *Index* as 3825) in Grimestone's preaching-book (*CB XIV*, No. 68) has a weak addition, spoken by the 'spuse dere'. The poem's background and relationships are discussed by Rosemary Woolf in *RES*, N.S. xiii (1962), 9–10. It echoes two verses—Apoc. 3: 20 'ecce sto ad ostium et pulso' and Cant. 5: 2 'aperi mihi, soror mea, amica mea, columba mea, immaculata mea'. A similar verse is spoken by the wounded, victorious lover-knight in the 14th-century *Fasciculus Morum* (*Index* 498):

> Byholde my woundes how I am dight,
> For all ys wele and won in fight.
> I am forewoundyd—byholde my skyn
> And for my love thou lete me in!

which, as Miss Woolf shows, is introduced by two lines from Ovid's *Amores* (III. viii. 19–20) 'with a slight change in the second, so that what was in its original context a harsh reproach to Corinna that she should prefer an uncivilized soldier to the poet becomes an epitome of the lover-knight's complaint'. A very similar quatrain (*Index* 846) appears in MS. Bodley 649:

> For the I wax al rody opon the rode;
> Mi blod y scheedde to wasche in thi hert.
> Amende the betymes and seese of thi synne;
> Undo the dore of thin hert and let me inne.

Another variation appears in a 14th-century MS. (pr. Robbins, *Anglia*, lxxxiii (1965), 47):

> Deum ad cor intrare volentem excludunt:
> Sa longge ich have, lavedi, yhoved at thi gate,
> That mi fot is ifrore, faire lavedi, for thi luve faste to the stake.

NOTES

3. *lyvely.* The scribe's form probably represents *lefly/levely* 'lovable, lovely, delightful', or (possibly) *luvely* 'loving, lovable, beautiful'.

10–11. Cf. Cant. 5: 2 '. . . quia caput meum plenum est rore, et cincinni mei guttis noctium'.

42

Index 3228. 3. MS. e. 16th c. This poem may well be an adaptation of a secular love lyric. A carol (*EEC*, No. 27, Greene, *Sel.*, No. 58) with a burden beginning 'com home agayne' possibly echoes the same secular song. Religious adaptations or parodies of secular poems were common (see Woolf, App. J, 'Some Sixteenth-Century Parodies', pp. 407–11). The best-known 16th-century example is the adaptation of the song 'Come over the bourn, Bessy', which appears in a number of variant versions (*Index* 3318.4), one with as many as twelve stanzas, another with a single stanza and burden (Bodl., MS. Ashmole 176, f. 100^v):

> Come over the borne, Bessy,
> My litle pretye Bessy,
> > Come over the borne, Bessye, to me.
> Come over the borne, Bessy,
> My lytle pretye Bessye,
> > Come over the borne, Bessye, to me.
>
> .　　.　　.　　.　　.　　.
>
> This borne ys the world blynd,
> And Bessye she ys mankynd;
> > So pretye can I none fynd as she.
> She daunceth, she lepeth;
> [Christl] standeth and clepeth　　　　　　[*MS.* thurgh
> > 'Come over the borne, Bessye, to me!

A 15th-century lyric 'Trewlove trewe, on you I truste' (*CB XV*, No. 110), an appeal of Christ to man, is so close to secular love poetry that as Woolf (p. 187) points out, if it were not for the MS. rubric 'querimonia Xi languentis pro amore', we could well read it as a secular lyric.

43

Index 1463. The MS. (l. 15th c.) also contains some poems by Lydgate. This lyric occurs also in the earlier MS. Lambeth 853 (see No. 63 note). There is a study of the texts of this lyric and No. 61 in an unpub. B.Phil.

thesis by Felicity J. Riddy, 'A textual and literary study of the two versions of "Quia amore langueo"' (1965), English Library, Oxford. (Though the two lyrics share a refrain, they are not by the same poet—No. 61 was written in a more northerly dialect.) This lyric is bold and successful in its use of images from the Song of Songs and the theme of Christ the Lover-Knight. Cf. Woolf, pp. 187–91.

1 ff. An imaginative adaptation of the traditional 'chanson d'aventure' opening, common in both secular and religious lyrics (see Sandison), in which the poet rides out and overhears a dialogue, a plaint, etc.

3. *treulofe*: here possibly the flower? (cf. *Sir Gawain and the Green Knight*, ed. N. Davis (Oxford, 1968), l. 612 note)—the poet in fact finds a 'true love'.

8. *quia amore langueo*: cf. Cant. 2: 5, 5: 8. It is a favourite phrase in devotional literature; cf. Rolle's *Form of Living* (ed. Horstmann, *Yorkshire Writers. Richard Rolle of Hampole* (London, 1895), i. 29) and *Index* 830, 1332. See also No. 61.

9–12. This scene suggests very strongly (see Woolf, p. 188) the devotional image of 'Christ in Distress' (*Christus im Elend*) which portrays the wounded Christ sitting beneath the cross. See G. von der Osten, 'Job and Christ', *Warburg Journal*, xvi (1958), 153–8 (Job sitting *in sterquilinio* is sometimes taken as a figure of the suffering Christ).

21. It is difficult to choose between the readings of the two MSS. here. C.'s *place* sounds like a substitution, but the word can mean 'palace' (cf. No. 60. 13).

25 ff. Cf. the 'reproaches' which Christ makes in the complaints (e.g. No. 29, etc.)

28. *surcote*: the more obviously knightly word, common in romance ('an outer garment worn over the armour'), seems preferable here to L.'s *scherte*, although this does occur in other versions of the lover-knight story (cf., e.g., Henryson's *The Bludy Serk*).

41 ff. Cf. No. 30 and note.

57 ff. The image of the wound in Christ's side as a nest or refuge is not uncommon in devotional literature. Cf. St. Bernard (*Sermo lxi in Cantica*, PL clxxxiii. 1071–2) on the text 'columba mea in foraminibus petrae' (Cant. 2: 14), where the *foramina petrae* are taken to be the wounds of Christ. (Cf. *NQ*, N.S. 10, ccviii (1963), 85.)

68. *dawngerouse*: 'disdainful, reluctant', a word full of associations of *fine amour*. On 'daunger' in the courtly tradition, see C. S. Lewis, *The Allegory of Love*, pp. 364–6.

70. *myn armes ben spred*: cf. the poem 'Sweet Jesu, now wol I synge' (*Index* 3238), ed. Horstmann, *Yorkshire Writers*, ii, p. 15, ll. 181–4:

Jesu, of love I seo tokenyng—
Thin armes spradde to love-cluppyng,
Thin hed bouwede to swete cussyng,
Thi syde al opene to love-schewyng.

86 L.'s *crippe*, the rarer form, is perhaps more likely to represent the original then C.'s *skrypp* (Riddy).

105 ff. On the image of Christ as mother, see Woolf, pp. 189–90, and A. Cabassut, 'Une dévotion médiévale peu connue, la dévotion à "Jésus notre mère"', *Revue d'ascétique et de mystique*, xxv (1949), 234–45, 'God is our Mother', *Life of the Spirit*, ii. 15 (1945), 49–53. In ME it receives its fullest treatment in chapter 60 of Julian of Norwich's *Revelations of Divine Love*.

44

Index 611. This poem is preserved in three 14th-c. MSS. (see the discussion in *CB XIV*, pp. 273–4). In the Hunterian MS. (l. 14th c.) this poem follows another lyric on the love of Jesus, 'Jesu swete is the love of thee' (No. 47). It is an impressive, if loosely organized, dramatic treatment of the theme of the compelling power of love (the theme of the *De laude caritatis* of Hugh of St. Victor). See the discussion of the poem and its background by Woolf, pp. 166–8. It echoes the *Philomena* of John of Howden. The contrarieties and the violent paradoxical behaviour of love is a theme found in other religious lyrics (see Woolf, pp. 169–72, and see especially *CB XIV*, Nos. 66, 84); it owes much to the treatment of the theme in secular literature, which is of great antiquity (see E. P. M. Dronke, 'The Conclusion of *Troilus and Criseyde*', *MÆ* xxxiii (1964), 50 and note, E. Wind, *Pagan Mysteries in the Renaissance* (2nd ed., London, 1967), pp. 161–5).

14. *it hath no lawe*: proverbial. Cf. *Knight's Tale* (*C.T.* A ll. 1163 ff.) where Arcite quotes the 'olde clerkes sawe': 'who shal yeve ɔ lovere any lawe?' One of the 'clerks' is Boethius, in his account of Orpheus and Eurydice (*De Consolatione Philosophiae*, III, metrum 12). For later examples see M. P. Tilley, *A Dictionary of the Proverbs in England in the sixteenth and seventeenth centuries* (Ann Arbor, Mich., 1950), L 508.

15 ff. On early devotion to the Sacred Heart of Christ, see L. Gougaud, *Dévotions et pratiques ascétiques du Moyen Âge*, pp. 74–128.

34. *of day the nyght*. The other two MSS. have *day of (the) nyght*, which is hardly consistent with the following line. Carleton Brown's suggestion, that we have here an allusion to the darkness from the sixth to the ninth hour, seems most likely.

39–40. MS. *is maad* makes rather forced sense: 'everyone knows that Love is united with Christ.' *Hath maad*: 'and (in addition to Mary and John) everyone who has been united to Christ by Love knows that "so inliche love nas nevere noon".'

45

Index 1930. On the MS. see No. 19 note.
7 ff. Cf. No. 19, ll. 21–4 note.

46

Jesu be thou my joy: *Index* 1664.5. A tag from Rolle's *English Psalter* (MS. 15th c.). The ecstatic 'love-longing' expressed by this and the following lyrics is characteristic of Rolle's work (see Woolf, pp. 169–72). Cf. the lyric at the end of *Ego Dormio*:

> My sange es in syhtyng, my lyfe es in langynge,
> Til I the se, my keyng, so fayre in thi schynyng,
> So fayre in thi fayrehede . . .

Jesu, my luf, my joy, my reste: *Index* 1735. MS. Add. 37049 is a 15th-c. miscellany of religious pieces, probably written in a Carthusian house, in which the influence of Rolle is very evident. In the MS. this verse is accompanied by a picture of Christ showing his wounds, and a cleric praying below. The first lines of this verse appear in stanza two of another prayer in MS. Harley 2406 (*Index* 1771):

> Jesus, my joye, my love, my rest,
> Thy perfyte love close in my brest,
> That I the love and nevere rest
> Or make myn hert in peces to brest.

47

Index 1747. MS. also contains No. 44. There are two longer versions of this poem, and in the longer piece 'Swete Jesu now wol I synge' (*Index* 3238) it has been combined with a similar lyric 'Swete Jesu, king of blisse' (No. 48). The opening is based on the famous poem *Jesu dulcis memoria* (*OBMLV* No. 233), formerly attributed to St. Bernard (see A. Wilmart, *Le 'Jubilus' dit de st-Bernard* (Rome, 1944)), which is also echoed in No. 44 and in 'Swete Jesu now wol I synge'. The Sarum

Primer of 1536 has an elaborately aureate version. On the devotion to the
Holy Name of Jesus, see Woolf, pp. 172–9, and A. Cabassut, 'La dévo-
tion au nom de Jésus dans l'Église d'Occident', *La Vie spirituelle*, lxxxvi
(1952), 46–69. This is now usually associated with the name of St.
Bernardino of Siena (1380–1444), but it was popular earlier in England.
It is a marked feature of the work of Rolle and some other mystical
writers. Cf. also this verse by Herebert (*Index* 3632.6):

> Thys nome ys also on honikomb, that yyfth ous savour and swetnesse,
> And hyt ys a seollich nome, that maketh ous wondren hys heynesse,
> And hyt ys on holsom nome, that bryng[t]h ous bote of wykkenesse,
> And hyt ys a nome of lyf, that bryngth ous joie and gladsomnesse.

48

Index 3236. MS. Digby 86 (1272–82) was copied in the diocese of
Worcester (see *CB XIII*, pp. xxviii–xxxv, and the full discussion by
B. D. H. Miller, 'The Early History of Bodleian MS. Digby 86', *Annuale
Mediaevale* (Duquesne Studies), iv (1963), 23–56). Besides Latin and
French pieces it contains an important collection of English lyrics and
poems. There is a longer version of this poem (15 stanzas) in MS.
Harley 2253. See Woolf, p. 174.

49

Index 1733. MS. 14th c. Possibly the work of Richard Rolle: see B. D.
Brown, *Bodleian Quarterly Record*, vii, No. 73 (1932), 4–5.

50

These two tags (*Index* 1758.5, 1002) introduce a series of verse prayers
addressed to Christ. For the image of the wounded heart of Christ as
a refuge, see No. 43, ll. 57 ff. and note.

51

Index 1727. Merton College MS. 204 was written in 1446–9 by John
Gisburgh. This seems to have been one of the most popular of all ME
religious lyrics. It is based on an earlier poem (*Index* 1752, *CB XIV*,
No. 94), and of the two poems together no fewer than 24 MS. copies
are known. The poem and its author, Richard de Caistre, the vicar of

St. Stephen's, Norwich (d. 1420), are discussed by the Revd. Dundas Harford (*Norfolk and Norwich Archaeological Society*, xvii (1908–10), 221–44) and *CB XV*, pp. 313–14.

41–2. Cf. Eph. 2:20.

52

Index 2471. The MS. (15th c.) contains a number of English verse prayers.

53

A series of short prayers addressed to Christ. On this type of lyric see Robbins, 'Popular Prayers in ME verse', *MP* xxxvi (1939), 337–50, 'Private Prayers in ME Verse', *SP* xxxvi (1939), 466–75.

(*a*) Not recorded in *Index*. It seems to be a variant of *Index* 1684 (*CB XIV*, No. 52). MS. Lyell 30 (completed in 1441) contains a number of English devotional poems. For a full description, see Albinia de la Mare, *Catalogue of Medieval MSS. bequeathed to the Bodleian Library, Oxford, by James P. R. Lyell* (Oxford, 1971), pp. 61–74.

(*b*) *Index* 1703. (MS. *c.* 1500; private prayers for a member of the Talbot family.) A very popular prayer by the Holy Name of Jesus; the *Index* lists 18 versions. What seems to be a fragment of it is found carved on a piece of wood (formerly the outside of a seat) at Warkworth Church near Banbury (see *NQ*, N.S. 14, ccxii (1967), 131). The quatrain is often followed by two further lines which vary from version to version (in this MS.: 'And bryng us to thy blysse / that never shall have ende / Swete Jesu Amen.').

(*c*) *Index* 1700.5. A prayer to Christ by the Precious Blood. For a later example, cf. the lines written (very unclearly) in a 1546 *Primer* (Bodl., 4° P 16 Th. Seld.):

> O lorde, lett thy bludde my raunsum be,
> And for thy (?) [marsy be] clene. Wasshe me—
> My fleshe withowte, my soule withyn,
> My fleshe from fellthe, my soule from syn.

The Precious Blood was a popular subject in late medieval devotion. Various monasteries and churches claimed to possess particles, notably at Bruges, Fécamp, and, in England, Ashridge and Hailes (the phial of the 'Blood of Hailes', by which Chaucer's Pardoner swears, was presented to the monks by Edmund, Earl of Cornwall, in 1270).

(*d*) *Index* 1729. A private prayer to be said at the Levation of the Host (on this common type see Robbins, 'ME Verse Levation Prayers', *MP* xl (1942) 131–46). The type still occurs in e. 16th-century *Horae*, cf.

A prayer to be sayd at the levacyon of the sacrament.

> Hayle very body, incarnate of a virgyn,
> Nayled on a crosse, and offred for mannes syne,
> Whose syde beynge percyd, blode ran out plentuously!
> At the poynte of deathe let us receyve the bodely,
> O swete, o holy, o Jesu, sonne of Mary.
>
> (Bodl. Douce BB 231, f. 83)

Cf. *The Lay-Folks Mass-Book*, ed. T. F. Simmons (EETS lxxi (1879)), pp. 38–41, 283–8.

(e) *Index* 1571; for MS. cf. No. 48 note. Similar English prayers based on Christ's words (Luke 23: 46) are *Index* 1600, 1952. The Latin words ('in manus tuas commendo spiritum meum') are used as a prayer before sleep, or at the hour of death (cf., in a serious context, *Havelok* 228, in a comic, *Reeve's Tale* A 4287).

54

Index 1707, followed (ll. 54–end) by *Index* 1711. MS. first half 15th c. In the MS. the piece is preceded by this rubric: 'Here men may see hou oure lord Jesu Crist schadde his precious blood vii tymes ayens the vii deedli synnes, of whiche the firste is this . . .' For similar prayers which set the 'sheddings' of Christ's blood against the seven deadly sins, see *CB XIV*, No. 123, *CB XV*, No. 62. On the general background to this type of poem, see *NQ* N.S. 10, ccviii (1963), 128, Woolf pp. 225–6, F. Wormald, 'The Revelation of the Hundred Pater Nosters', *Laudate*, xiv (1936), 165–82. It was a popular subject of late medieval devotion (the list of 'sheddings' varies, but normally begins with the circumcision).

55

Index 420. MS. 15th c. This remarkable little poem, in a Latin homily suggests a scene from romance, such as a meeting with an Otherworld *fée*; some of the ideas and images (e.g. *bote of bale*, the 'bond of love') are found in secular love poetry. See Peter Dronke, *The Medieval Lyric* (London, 1968), pp. 69–70. But it is *trewe love* which can be found in this maiden who stands at the place where mankind's *bale* was cured. The *sprynge-wel* is identified by the homilist with the side of Christ (the wound in the side is often called *well* or *fons*, cf. No. 35), the maiden is the Virgin Mary (*puella stans est beata Maria virgo*). The poem is used here to introduce two further love-lyrics addressed to the Virgin.

56

Index 1836. For MS. see No. 8 (b) note.

13 ff. The 'sweet eyes' of the Virgin, and the suppliant's prayer for a glance, are often found in Marian poetry. Cf. *Salve Regina*: 'Eia ergo, advocata nostra, illos tuos misericordes oculos ad nos converte', or Ryman's poems:

> Here in this vale of care and woo,
> Sith thou art oure mediatrise,
> Thyn eyen of mercy, of grace alsoo,
> Turne thou to us in mercyfull wyse. . . . (*EEC*, No. 214)

> . . . Sweete and benigne mediatrise,
> Thyn eyen of grace on us thou cast,
> Sith thou art quene of Paradise. . . .   (*EEC*, No. 215)

The Bible often uses the image of turning the eyes (or face) towards or away from a person as a sign of favour or disfavour (cf. Isa 1: 15, Ps. 131 (Vg.): 10, etc.). But Marian poetry also frequently and deliberately invests the image with the suggestions of secular love-poetry, in which the lady's eyes, and the joy which a loving glance from them can bring to the poet, are favourite topics. Cf. Bernard de Ventadour (ed. C. Appel, (Halle, 1915), 17. 41-4):

> Negus jois al meu no s'eschai,
> Can ma domna·m garda ni·m ve,
> Que'l seus bels douz semblans me vai
> Al cor, que m'adous' e·m reve

('No joy equals mine when my lady sees me and looks upon me; then to my heart goes her sweet fair glance which fills me with sweetness and refreshes me'). There is a striking use of the image in *Paradiso* iv, 139-42:

> Beatrice mi guardò con li occhi pieni
> di faville d'amor così divini,
> che, vinta, mia virtute diè le reni,
> e quasi mi perdei con li occhi chini

('Beatrice looked at me with eyes so full of the sparkling of love and so divine that my power, overcome, took flight, and, with eyes cast down, I was almost lost' (Sinclair)).

57

Index 456. MS. 15th c. (written by more than one hand; contains various ME poems, including *Degaré*). This is a longer and more elaborate love-poem to the Virgin Mary, which makes use of the themes and diction of courtly lyric. The final envoy suggests that the poet had in mind the fashionable verse love-epistles of the period (see Robbins, *Secular Lyrics*, Nos. 189 ff., and p. 286, N. Davis, 'The *Litera Troili* and English Letters', *RES*, N.S. xvi (1965), 233–44). The envoy has some verbal similarities with the poem 'Goe lyttyll bill' (*CB XV*, No. 46), which achieves such a nice balance between 'secular' and 'divine' love that it is difficult to know whether it is addressed to the Virgin or to the poet's mistress. The acrostic on the name Maria is found in other poems of this type (see *CB XV*, No. 31, *EEC*, No. 180, Dreves, xxxi, Nos. 125 ff.). It illustrates both the intense veneration in which the name of Mary was held (see Woolf, p. 291, P. Vinc van Wijk, *De Naam Maria* (Leiden, 1936)) and a tendency towards a rather arid formalism. Dreves xxxi contains some extraordinary examples, cf. (No. 127):

> . . . Margarita mundans mentes,
> Mater mitigans maerentes,
> Mel misericordiae,
> Aula agni, Abel ara,
> Arbor auferens amara,
> Ales alimoniae . . .

Chaucer's Marian *ABC* (from the French of de Guilleville) is a more successful example of a related type, the 'alphabetical' poem.

29 ff. A popular subject of romance; cf. *The Squire of Low Degree*, ll. 1–2:

> It was a squer of lowe degre
> That loved the kings doughter of Hungre . . .

46. *pentafiloun*: cinquefoil, the plant *potentilla*. Cf. the *Grete Herball* (1529): 'Pentafilon is an herbe called fyve-leved. For pentha in greke is .v. & filo is lefe. . . . It groweth in sandy places and medowes. It bereth fyve leves on a stalke and hath yelowe floures & stretcheth on the grounde.' It is commended as a remedy for 'the payne of the joyntes

that cometh of strokes or travayll', 'ache of the wombe caused of coleryke humours', 'agaynst rottennesse of the gommes', 'bledynge of the nose', 'agaynst bytyng of serpentes', and 'cankers'. Cf. also the OE *Herbarium Apuleii*, ed. O. Cockayne, *Leechdoms, Wortcunning and Starcraft of Early England* (London, 1864), pp. 86–9.

50 ff. Each letter of the name Maria is associated with an Old Testament 'figure' of the Virgin, and with a stone with symbolic properties. In spite of the reference in l. 87, it is not clear that the poet had any particular lapidary in mind (on lapidaries, see Joan Evans, *Magical Jewels* (Oxford, 1922), J. Evans and Mary S. Serjeantson, *English Medieval Lapidaries*, EETS cxc, P. Studer and J. Evans, *Anglo-Norman Lapidaries* (Paris, 1924)).

51. *Mychell*: Michal, the younger of Saul's daughters (see 1 Sam. (Vg. 1 Reg.) 14: 49, 2 Sam. 3: 13–14). For a picture of her lowering David from the wall in the *Biblia Pauperum*, cf. E. M. Thompson, *Bibliographica*, iii (1897).

55–6. The pearl was a traditional symbol of purity (cf., e.g., *Pearl*, ed. E. V. Gordon (Oxford, 1953), pp. xxvi ff.).

56. *Abigaill*: see 1 Sam. 25: 3–42. St. Bonaventura (*Sermo iv de Nativitate B.V.M.*, *Opera* (Quaracchi, 1882–1902), ix. 712) mentions her as a figure of Mary: 'fuit etiam mulier speciosa; unde figuratur per Abigail.'

61–3. *the adamauntt*. From antiquity, the name *adamas* denoted three things: originally, a very hard metal, perhaps steel; a very hard stone, like corundum or diamond; a stone that attracts iron or steel (cf. Donne, *Holy Sonnets, Divine Poems*, ed. H. Gardner, p. 13: 'and thou like Adamant draw mine iron heart'), the mineral magnetite (Albertus Magnus, *Book of Minerals*, tr. Dorothy Wyckoff (Oxford, 1967), pp. 70–1). Cf. Evans and Serjeantson, *English Medieval Lapidaries*, pp. 14, 15, 37, 66–7.

64. *Rachel*: see Gen. 29 f. She is commonly used as a figure of the Virgin Mary, cf. (among many examples) *CB XIV*, No. 32, ll. 53–4:

> Thou ert the ryghte vayre Rachel,
> Fayrest of alle wymman.

65. *the ruby* is highly praised by the lapidaries: 'the gentil ruby fyn and red is the lord of all precyous stones and gemme of gemmes, and he has the vertus of all stones' (Evans and Serjeantson, pp. 41–2, 28–9, 48–9, etc.).

71. *Judith*. The story (from an apocryphal book of the Old Testament) of Judith's deliverance of Israel from the tyrant Holofernes was

very popular throughout the Middle Ages. She is commonly taken as a figure of the Virgin Mary, cf. *EEC*, No. 209:

> O stronge Judith, so full of myght,
>   By thy vertu we be made fre,
> For thou hast putte oure foo to flyght,
>   *Mater misericordie.*

73. *jaspid*: the jasper, a bright-coloured chalcedony, 'the most esteemed being of a green colour'. Cf. Studer and Evans, pp. 81–2: 'Home maintent et ben conforte . . . / Home defent et fet puissant'; it is 'ful gode ayens temptacion of fendes, of Jewes, and Sarazins' (Evans and Serjeantson, pp. 23–4; cf. pp. 43–4, 93–4, etc.). The lady Annot in one of the Harley lyrics is likened to 'jasper the gentil that lemeth with lyht' (*CB XIII*, No. 76).

82. *Abisaag*: Abishag, the beautiful Shunammite who served David in his old age; cf. 1 Kings 1: 1–4. St. Bonaventura (*Sermo II de Annuntiatione, Opera*, ix. 660a) says 'non est dubium, quia per David Christum, per eius pueros Angelos, per Abisag Virginem Mariam intelligere debeamus, quae ratione virginalis decoris ad regem adducta est, ut non solum ministraret, sed etiam foveret, concipiendo et nutriendo'.

allatory: alectorius < Lat. *gemma alectoria*, 'cock-stone' (Gk. ἀλέκτωρ 'cock'), a small crystal thought to grow in a capon's womb. It brought victory, made a man well spoken of and loved; it was good for women in childbirth, and helped them to find favour in the eyes of their lords (see Evans and Serjeantson pp. 31, 51, 59, 67–8, 124; Studer and Evans, p. 33).

58

Index 1041.5. MS. third quarter 15th c. The stanza occurs separately here (on the end flyleaf), but is really a version of the first stanza of *Index* 897, a translation of *Gaude flore virginali* in seven stanzas (ed. Furnivall, EETS xv, pp. 174–5). Other ME versions are *Index* 1804 (*CB XV*, No. 36) and 1807. Cf. also *CB XV*, Nos. 34, 35. A version of the Latin text is printed in Daniel, *Thes.* i, p. 346. The hymn is found in early 16th-century *Horae*. Cf. MS. Bodl. Douce BB 231 (f. 79ᵛ):

> Rejoyse, O floure of virgyns all
> In thyne honoure and grace especyall
>   Excedynge a thowsande folde
> The pryncypalyte of aungelles eminent
> And the dygnyte of sayntes refulgent
>   More than can be tolde . . .

59

Index 2415. MS. C.U.L. Ee. 1.12 (1490–1500) is a collection of English songs, carols, and translations of Latin hymns by the Franciscan James Ryman, a prolific if not very talented writer. (Almost all of the contents are printed by Zupitza, *Archiv*, lxxxix. 167–338; the carols are to be found in *EEC*.) In this poem, the Latin refrains are from the antiphon *Regina caeli laetare* (Daniel, *Thes*. ii, pp. 319–20), which is attested from the late 12th century. The Franciscans were apparently using it as a seasonal antiphon by 1249. There are a number of other ME versions and expansions. See, e.g., *CB XV*, Nos. 27–9, *EEC*, Nos. 185, 186, and (by Ryman) 189, 218.

60

Index 3225. MS. Cotton Caligula A ii (15th c.) contains a number of English romances and poems. This lyric occurs in two other MSS. The poets and artists of the Middle Ages were fond of the image of the Virgin Mary as the Queen of Heaven; the richness of colour and the swinging censers of the 'Notre Dame de la belle verrière' at Chartres have their equivalents in rich verbal descriptions. Cf. the 13th-century *On God Ureisun of Ure Lefdi* (*CB XIII*, No. 3):

> . . . Heih is thi kinestol onuppe cherubine,
> Bivoren thine leove sune withinnen seraphine.
> Murie dreameth engles bivoren thin onsene,
> Pleieth and sweieth and singeth bitweonen . . .

In celebrating the Assumption and the Coronation of the Virgin the later poets often employed grandiloquent 'aureate' diction. This lyric makes use of some lines from the Song of Songs which, as Carleton Brown points out, were used as the antiphon for Vespers on the Feast of the Assumption (*York Breviary*, Surtees Soc. lxxv. 476):

tota pulchra es amica mea: et macula non est in te: favus distillans labia tua: mel et lac sub lingua tua: odor unguentorum tuorum super omnia aromata: jam enim hyems transiit: imber abiit et recessit: flores apparuerunt: vinee florentes odorem dederunt: et vox turturis audita est in terra nostra: surge propera amica mea: veni de Libano: veni coronaberis.

9. *cage*: ? 'a scaffold, elevated stage or seat' (*OED*, s.v. *cage* sb. I, 4 b, *MED*, 3 (a)). Can the poet be thinking of the sort of elevated throne he may have seen in a mystery play? His use of the phrase

columba mea in l. 10 perhaps suggests a playful and affectionate pun. If this sense is possible, the L.H. reading in l. 15 may be defended as a *difficilior lectio* against Cotton's more obvious *herytage*.

10. *columba mea*: cf. Cant. 2: 14.

28. *ayeyn my ryghtes*: 'contrary to my laws', apparently a reference to the miraculous nature of the bodily Assumption.

33. *myn*: (?) *pron.* = my kindred, my saints, (?) *v.* = go (cf. OED *min v*[1].

44. Apparently an attempt to imitate the imagery of the Song of Songs, cf., e.g., 4: 3, 7: 7–8. The reading of the Harley MS., 'with braunchis and flouris of swete smelle', seems to have smoothed out the sense at the expense of the rhyme.

57. *pulchra ut luna*: cf. Cant. 6: 9.

61

Index 1460. MS. Second half 15th c. (contains devotional treatises, prayers, and poems). This poem was obviously popular; eight more or less complete versions are recorded. MS. Douce 322 has the most complete text, but it does not represent (*CB XIV*) 'its original form' (cf. the study by Mrs. Riddy—see No. 43 note)—there are indications (e.g. the forms *bus* (l. 15), wald/tald/called (ll. 58 ff.), etc.) that it was written in a more northerly dialect. In B.M. MS. Add 37049 it is accompanied by some rather crude illustrations. In the largest, a crowned Virgin stands holding the Christ child in a 'tabernacle of a tower'; beneath, a kneeling monk prays:

> O Maria the flowre of virgyns clere
> In al oure nede oure prayer thou here.

See the discussion of the poem by Woolf, pp. 301–2.

1. *tabernacle*: 'a canopied niche or recess in a wall or pillar, to contain an image' (*OED*, s.v. *tabernacle*, sb. 4. b).

2. *musyng on the mone*. The moon was sometimes associated with the Virgin Mary. Cf. the phrase *pulchra ut luna* (Cant. 6: 9) used in No. 60, l. 57. A verse in the Apocalypse (12: 1) 'Et signum magnum apparuit in caelo: mulier amicta sole, et luna sub pedibus eius, et in capite ejus corona stellarum duodecim' was also applied to the Virgin. The idea is sometimes given visual form: a prose prayer to Mary in MS. Arundel 285 is accompanied by a woodcut of 'a rayed Virgin, standing on a crescent moon with the Christ child in her arms' (*Devotional Pieces in Prose and Verse*, ed. J. A. W. Bennett, p. xxxiv). Cf. H. Rahner, *Greek Myths and Christian Mystery* (Eng. tr., London, 1963), pp. 154–63.

8. *quia amore langueo*: see No. 43, l. 8 note.

35. *gete*. Some MSS. have the more obvious *geve*, but *gete* makes quite precise theological sense: 'obtain for thee'.

52–6. The Virgin addresses these lines to Christ.

62

Index 1077. On MS. see No. 39 note.

63

Index 1032. MS. Lambeth 853 (e. 15th c.) contains an important collection of devotional verse, including, for example, versions of Nos. 43, 60, 61. This lyric occurs in its complete version in three other MSS. The copies show much variation. It is an elaborate expansion of the antiphon (first found in the 12th c.): 'Ave regina caelorum, ave domina angelorum, salve radix sancta ex qua mundo lux est orta; gaude gloriosa, super omnes speciosa. Vale, valde decora, et pro nobis semper Christum exora.' (See Daniel, *Thes.* ii, p. 319, Dom B. Capelle, *Les Questions liturgiques et paroissiales*, xxxi (Mar. 1950), 33–5.) There are other ME versions; cf. *Index* 2610 (*CB XV*, No. 24) and *Index* 1056 (Lydgate's 'Hayle luminary and benign lanterne', EETS cvii, p. 291). A number of other lyrics which use the anaphora of 'Hail' are adaptations or expansions of the *Salve regina*. The obvious weakness of this type of lyric is a dull and uninspired handling of the catalogue of exclamations; very few approach even remotely the virtuosity and the dynamic force of Dunbar's *Ane Ballet of Our Lady*.

15. *pinacle in hevene*. The word *pinacle* is used of the Virgin in the Advocates MS. version of No. 5. (l. 4) 'that holy pynakell preved of price'. While it means something like 'the culmination or point of perfection' (*OED*), it has perhaps something of the literal sense—one of the traditional figures of the Virgin is the 'tower of David'.

20. *In temynge*: the Virgin's care for women in childbirth was traditional. 'Our Lady's bonds' was an old term for pregnancy or confinement. Noah's wife in the Towneley play swears by 'Mary that lowsid me of my bandis'.

29. *spice*: see No. 5, l. 5 note.

39. *tabernacle of the trynyte*: Mary is sometimes called the 'chamber' of the Trinity (e.g. *CB XIV*, No. 32), or the 'bower' or 'couch' of the Trinity, cf.

Salve mater pietatis
et totius trinitatis
nobile triclinium.
(Mone, ii, No. 524)

Cf. *PPl.* (B) XVI, 90 ff.:

And thanne spakke *Spiritus Sanctus* in Gabrieles mouthe,
To a mayde that highte Marye, a meke thinge with-alle,
That one Jesus, a justice sone moste jouke in her chambre,
Tyl *plenitudo temporis* fully comen were,
That Pieres fruit floured and fel to be ripe.

64

This poem is listed in the *Index* separately as 2478.8, but it is in fact a version of the Lydgatian piece 'O sterre of Jacob' (*Index* 2556), which occurs in four other MSS. It is a prayer to the Virgin Mary by the Five Joys (here the Annunciation, Nativity, Resurrection, Ascension, and Assumption), and is obviously intended to be read or said before retiring at night (another evening prayer to the Virgin, 'Upon my ryght syde y me laye', is printed in *CB XV*, No. 127). The Five Joys of the Virgin are celebrated in many songs, hymns,. and carols (see, for instance, *CB XIII*, Nos. 18, 41, *CB XIV*, Nos. 11, 31, *CB XV*, Nos. 30, 31, *EEC*, Nos. 230 f.). In others the number of the Joys is put at seven or fifteen. See the discussion of the theme by Woolf, pp. 134–43, 297–302. There are a number of formal orisons similar to this (cf., e.g., *CB XIV*, Nos. 26, 122) and a couple of short prayers, *Index* 1837 and 2099; the latter is a popular prayer tag (see Robbins, *MP* xxxvi. 348) which is used as a *titulus* in a wall-painting of the Life of the Virgin at Broughton Church near Banbury, Oxon.

65

Index 3477.6. MS. Reid 7 (15th c.) is a copy of the Sarum Hours written in France, possibly at Rouen, to which some English prayers have been added (see N. R. Ker, *Medieval Manuscripts in British Libraries* (Oxford, 1969), i, p. 379, and cf. also *Burlington Magazine*, i (1903), 389). This lyric is a translation of *Stella celi extirpavit*, an anthem to the Virgin Mary praying for her protection against the plague.

The Black Death came to England first in 1348, and recurred with varying intensity throughout the later Middle Ages. It was the occasion of a small and curious class of works of art and literature. Mary is sometimes represented sheltering the faithful beneath her protecting mantle from the javelins of the plague cast on them by God (see E. Mâle, *L'Art religieux de la fin du Moyen Âge en France* (2nd ed., Paris, 1949), pp. 200–1, P. Perdrizet, *La Vierge de miséricorde* (Paris, 1908), pp. 107–49). There are many crudely drawn or printed popular images of favourite 'plague saints' such as St. Sebastian or St. Roch (see P. Heitz and W. L. Schreiber, *Pestblätter des 15. Jahrhunderts* (Strasbourg, 1901)). There was a special Mass against the plague, and there are a number of prayers, poems, and didactic works of a medical or pseudo-medical nature (cf. R. H. Bowers, 'A Middle English Mnemonic Plague Tract', *Southern Folklore Quarterly*, xx (1956), 118–25, or Lydgate's *Doctryne for the Pestilence*). There are longer poems in English in the 15th century (see *CB XV*, Nos. 135, 136, R. Kaiser, *Medieval English* (3rd ed., Berlin, 1958), p. 509). Ryman has a version of the *Stella celi extirpavit* in two stanzas (*Index* 3374); Lydgate has two (EETS, ES cvii, pp. 294–6); another occurs in early 16th-century *Horae*. See Woolf, pp. 282–3. The best of the English verse prayers against the plague is Henryson's *Ane Prayer for the Pest*.

66

Index 1786.5. A prayer in a 15th-century hand on an originally blank page (f. 107ᵛ) in the sumptuous 'Talbot Hours', now in the Fitzwilliam Museum. The volume was written in France for John Talbot, Earl of Shrewsbury (1388?–1453), the famous English military commander, 'ducum Angliae omnium strenuissimus at audacissimus' (the 'brave Talbot' of *1 Henry VI*). The exploits of 'le roi Talabot' became legendary. After his death his body was brought back to England, and interred in the church of Whitchurch, Shropshire. There is a 15th-century portrait of him at Compton Wynyates. The poem invokes the aid of three saints—the popular Catherine; Christopher, for Talbot's safe return; and George, traditionally associated with knighthood as well as with England (in Talbot's last attack on a camp near Castillon his men are said to have charged with the cry 'Talbot, Talbot, St. George!').

67

Index 2993. On the background of this 14th-century poem see R. H. Robbins, 'A Middle English Prayer to St. Mary Magdalen', *Traditio*, xxiv (1968), 458–64. Mary Magdalen was the object of an intense cult (see Helen Meredith Garth, *Saint Mary Magdalene in Medieval Literature*

(Baltimore, 1950), J. Szövefffy, '"Peccatrix quondam femina"', *Traditio,* xix (1963), 178–282, and references given by Robbins, p. 458). Her help is often invoked, as in this poem, for the penitent sinner. In ME there are a number of poems which narrate her life, and a play is based on her story (EETS lxx). One poem, printed in Thynne's *Chaucer* (1532), elaborates the concept of Mary Magdalen as the 'Weeper' (cf. the later poem by Crashaw), and gives her a long lamentation ('Plonged in the wawe of mortal distresse . . .', *Index* 2759). Cf. Woolf, RF, pp. 384–91.

68

Index 1049. By James Ryman (see No. 59 note), himself a Franciscan. It seems to be based on this prayer (Dreves, v, No. 61 (p. 178)), from a 15th-century Franciscan breviary: 'Salve sancte pater, patriae lux, norma minorum, Virtutis speculum, recti via, regula morum; Carnis ab exsilio duc nos ad regna polorum.'

69

Index 2393. A verse prayer to King Henry VI. In spite of his unfortunate political record, Henry was made by popular devotion into a saint and martyr. Henry VII asked the Pope for his formal canonization, but nothing came of it (possibly, it was suggested, because Henry VII was not prepared to pay the large fees demanded). Henry's saintly virtues are described in a work prepared by Blackman, his Carthusian chaplain (see M. R. James, *Henry the Sixth, A Reprint of John Blacman's Memoir* (English text only), Cambridge, 1919, 1955). He was a pious man, who wore simple garb, and often a hair-shirt under his splendid robes, said grace 'like a monk', and had on his table a dish with a representation of the Five Wounds. J. P. Collier (*Trevelyan Papers*, Camden Society, lxvii (1857), 53–60) prints another short English verse prayer to him (*Index* 333.5), and some Latin hymns and prayers. On his miracles and cult images, see *Henrici VI Angliae Regis Miracula Postuma,* ed. P. Grosjean (Brussels, 1935), *The Miracles of King Henry VI,* ed. R. Knox and S. Leslie (Cambridge, 1923). A very fine woodcut is reproduced as pl. xxxvii of Campbell Dodgson, 'English Devotional Woodcuts of the late fifteenth century', *Walpole Society*, xvii (1928–9), 95–108. The pious king re-appeared in Tudor pageants (cf. S. Anglo, *Spectacle, Pageantry, and Early Tudor Policy* (Oxford, 1969), pp. 38 ff.). Cf. McKenna, RF, pp. 72–88.

Naturally enough, there were in the Middle Ages a number of local cults of this type which did not lead to full canonization. Richard Rolle, the object of one of them (see Hope Emily Allen, *Writings Ascribed to Richard Rolle* (New York, 1927), pp. 51–61, 488–90) was a man of undoubted saintliness. Other cults (Simon de Montfort, Thomas of Lancaster) probably served a political as well as a religious purpose.

70

Index 2385. On MS. see No. 11 note. On the cult of guardian angels, see Dom A. Wilmart, *Auteurs spirituels et textes dévots* (Paris, 1932), pp. 537–58. There are a number of ME verse prayers to guardian angels (see *CB XV*, Nos. 132–4, R. H. Robbins, *MP* xxxvi (1939), 339, xl (1942), 142); cf. also the inscription in Campsal church (Yorkshire):

> .   .   .   .
>
> Bewar of the divyl when he blaws his horn
> And prai thy gode aungel convey the

(M. D. Anderson, *Drama and Imagery in English Medieval Churches* (Cambridge, 1963), p. 175). This lyric is a version of a Latin prayer to the guardian angel (*omni mane dicenda*) which was very popular in England (and in Scotland, cf. J. A. W. Bennett, *Devotional Pieces*) in the late Middle Ages (cf. Wilmart, pp. 554–7). The beginning—

> Angele qui meus es custos pietate superna
> Me tibi commissum salva, defende, guberna.
> Terge meam mentem vitiis et labe veterna
> Assiduusque comes michi sis viteque lucerna

—is based on some lines of Reginald of Canterbury (12th century) (cf. Dreves, l, No. 293, *OBMLV*, No. 145). The following lines of the prayer show variations. Wilmart notes a version in Wynkyn de Worde's Salisbury Primer (*c.* 1494) which has a quatrain

> O tu dulcis angele qui mecum moraris
> Licet personaliter mecum loquaris
> Animam cum corpore precor tuearis
> Iam hoc est officium ad quod assignaris

and a verset

> O beate angele nuncie dei nostri
> Actus meos regula ad votum dei altissimi.

This, or something like it, could well have been the original of the last three stanzas of the ME poem.

Index 496. MS. 15th c. The traditional paradoxes of the faith, that Christ is both God and Man, Mary both maiden and mother, that the Host seems to be bread but is flesh, are sometimes made into a simple sort of 'wit poetry'. These poems are sometimes single quatrains:

> Thow semest whyte and art red,
> Thow art flesche and semest bred;
> The farest myracle that ever was,
> To schew God and man in so lytyl space

(a variant of *Index* 1640 from Durham University MS. Cosin V. V. 19, f. 73ʳ); sometimes they are developed into quite elaborate carols or lyrics (see *CB XV*, Nos. 117–21, *EEC*, Nos. 282, 318–21). There is a riddling poem (*Index* 4111) on the *mirabilia* of the Bible:

> Who was ded ande never borne?
> —Adam that was oure first beforne.
> Who was borne and never deede?
> —Ennok and Ely that we of reed. . . .

In another (*Index* 4162.5) the list is stretched out over 29 quatrains. Yet another poem (*Index* 2503), which answers the questions it puts with the phrase *hoc factum est a Domino*, besides asking why all stars do not move in the same way, why Lot's wife was turned into a pillar of salt, etc., even ventures into contemporary *mirabilia*:

> How gat oure kyng the victory
>   At Agyncourt with a smal puissance?
> Who made Prynce Phelyp to flee
>   From Calice, with anger and myschaunce?
> Who wrought this worthy purviaunce—
>   The Scottis from Rokisburgh to go?
> Man, answere me without tariaunce,
>   *Hoc factum est a Domino.*

(In the stanza which follows, one of the marvels offended a Protestant reader, who has crossed through the lines

> He may as wele make brede and wyne
>   To turne into his flessh and to his bloode.)

For similar secular paradoxical and riddling verses, see Robbins, *Secular Lyrics of the 13th and 14th Centuries* (Oxford, 1952), No. 45 and p. 241, or the first ballad in Child's collection, 'Riddles Wisely Expounded'.

72

Index 37. The verse is written in a 16th-century hand on the flyleaf of the MS. A similar lyric (*Index* 4181) is sometimes attributed to Bishop Pecock at the time of his recantation in 1457, when he confessed that he had preferred his 'jugement and naturalle resoun before the Newe and Olde Testament, and the auctoryte and determinacioun of oure moder Hooly Churche':

> Witte hath wondir that resoun ne telle kan,
> How maidene is modir, and God is man.
> Leve thy resoun and bileve in the wondir,
> For feith is aboven and reson is under.

This seems to have been very popular: it occurs in 17 MSS., and was still remembered in the 17th century (see D. Gray, 'An Inscription at Hexham', *Archaeologia Aeliana*, 4th ser. xl (1962), 185–8).

73

Index 940. From the title-page of Pynson's *Hore Beate Marie Virginis* of 1514 (*STC* 15917). This prayer is found in a number of early 16th-century books of hours, and in one MS. copy. See the discussion by Curt F. Bühler, 'At thy golg first eut of the hous vlysse the saynge thus', *Studies in the Renaissance*, vi (1959), 223–7. The first occurrence of the English text seems to be in a Rouen book of hours from 1506, but a French version is attested earlier.

74

Index 2757.5, *STC* 22924. By William Cornish (cf. J. Stevens, *Musica Britannica*, xviii (1961)). The other songs are transcribed by Flügel, *Anglia*, xii (1889), 589 ff.

75

Index 3359. MS. Add. 34193 (l. 15th c.) contains a collection of translations of Latin hymns (see F. A. Patterson, 'Hymnal from MS. Add. 34193' in *Medieval Studies in Memory of Gertrude Schoepperle Loomis* (Paris, N.Y., 1927), pp. 443–88). This is a version of the *Ales diei nuncius* by Prudentius (taken from the *Cathemerinon (ad galli cantum)*). It is the only recorded ME version, but an Englishing of the hymn is found in early 16th-century Primers, e.g. the 1546 Henry VIII Primer:

> The byrde of day messinger
> Croweth and sheweth that lyght is nere:
> Christ the styrrer of the hert
> Woulde we shuld to lyfe convert.

> Upon Jesus let us cry,
> Wepyng, praiyng, sobrely,
> Devout prayer, meynt with wepe,
> Suffreth not pure hart to slepe.

> Christ shake of our hevy slepe,
> Breke the bondes of nyght so depe,
> Our olde synnes clense and skoure,
> Lyfe and grace unto us powre.

76

Index 2342. On MS. see No. 10 note.

77

The first of these tags (*Index* 995.3) occurs at the end of Rolle's *De Modo Vivendi*. The other (*Index* 3339) comes from the popular Franciscan preaching-book the *Fasciculus Morum* (on which see A. G. Little, *Studies in English Franciscan History* (Manchester, 1917), pp. 139–57, and F. Foster, 'A Note on the *Fasciculus Morum*', *Franciscan Studies*, viii (1948), 202–4). For the proverbial idea behind ll. 3–4, cf. *The Owl and the Nightingale*, ll. 405–8.

78

Index 3812. Late 15th c. MS. Douce 104 contains a copy of *Piers Plowman* (with illustrations); 'Tutivillus' is written at the end. Chattering in church (a vice usually attributed by anti-feminist writers to women) is often reproved. There are a number of admonitory stories of the type told by the Knight of Latour Landry (cf. T. Wright, EETS xxxiii, pp. 40–1): a hermit during mass looks at the ladies, knights, and squires who are jesting and 'jangling', 'and he beheld moche theyr contenaunce, and he sawe that at eche ere of man and woman was a fende, moche black and horryble, whiche also laughed and jangled amonge them, and wrote the words that were said. These fendes wenten spryngyng uppon theyr queynt arayement and nyce araye lyke as the smale byrdes that lepe fro braunche to braunche . . .' Cf. also J. E. Wells, *A Manual Of the Writings in Middle English 1050–1400* (New Haven, 1916), pp. 173, 234; G. R. Owst, *Literature and Pulpit* (revised ed., 1961), pp. 514–15; John of Garland, *Stella Maris*, ed. E. F. Wilson (Cambridge, Mass., 1946), p. 193 (story from Vincent of Beauvais). Another story has the devil carrying off in a sack the words 'overskipped' by clerks (cf. T. F. Crane, *The Exempla of Jacques de Vitry* (London, 1890), No. 19). Figures of the devil with his sack are found in wall-paintings and on misericords (see M. D. Anderson, *Drama and Imagery in English Medieval Churches*, pl. 24a, pp. 173–7). In the parish church of Old, Northants., there is part of a window showing a person with a devil (with rather gay red stripes) apparently sitting on his back. A scroll bears an inscription, now very unclear, which was read by the antiquarian John Bridges (*The History and Antiquities of Northamptonshire*, compiled . . . by P. Whalley (1791)) as:

> All claterers in the kyrght
> Schall hae yow for yowr warght.

On the name Tutivillus see *OED*, s.v. *Titivil* (the word later came to mean 'scoundrel' or 'tell-tale', with which meaning it is applied to Dunbar by Kennedy (*Flyting* 513)). Tutivillus appears as a lively character in the Towneley Doom Play (ed. G. England and A. W. Pollard, EETS, ES lxxi) and in the morality play *Mankind* (ed. F. J. Furnivall and A. W. Pollard, EETS, ES xci, pp. 18–22); in the *Myroure of Oure Ladye* (ed. J. H. Blunt, EETS, ES xix, p. 54) he says: 'I am a poure dyvel, and my name ys Tytyvyllus. . . . I muste eche day . . . brynge my master a thousande pokes full of faylynges, and of neglygences in syllables and wordes.'

79

The first piece is a short prayer (*Index* 1965) from Grimestone's preaching-book (cf. No. 15 note). The second (*Index* 1978) appears on f. 181ᵛ (present numbering) of New College MS. 88 (? c. 14th century), a collection of sermons. It is a simple prayer of contrition based on a passage from St. Augustine's *Confessions* VIII, c. 5:

Non erat quid responderem tibi veritate convictus dicenti mihi Surge qui dormis et exurge a mortuis et illuminabit tibi Christus nisi verba lenta et sompnolenta 'modo, ecce, modo. sine paululum'. Sed modo et modo non habebant modum, et sine paululum in longum ibat. Similiter est de differentibus penitencie.

Cf. the passage in Barclay's *Shyp of Folys* (ed. Jamieson (1874), i, pp. 162–5) 'Of them that prolonge from day to day to amende themselve' ('He that *cras, cras* syngeth with the crowe . . .'). There are a number of lyrics which express penitence or remorse for sin (cf. F. A. Patterson, *The Middle English Penitential Lyric* (New York, 1911)); the best are usually the most succinct, cf. C.U.L. MS. Ii. 3.8, f. 88ʳ (*Index* 141):

> Alas! Alas! Si haut, si bas!
> So lenger y leved so werchs yc was.
> Alas! alas! ibrocht ic am in perelus pas.
> Alas! alas! the game is ilore for lak of as.

80

Index 1454. On MS. Balliol 354 see No. 11 note. Longer versions of this poem appear in MS. Lambeth 853 and Trinity College, Cambridge, MS. 1450. See Rigg, pp. 51–2. The poem is a moral *chanson d'aventure* (cf. Sandison, pp. 81–93).

16. *revertere*: cf. *EEC*, Nos. 140, 269; Jer. 3: 1; Isa. 44: 22.

81

Index 1818; a verse from MS. Harley 2316 in a 14th-century hand. This sombre view of man's life is common in poems of the 'contemptus mundi' tradition. Cf. the lines in MS. Harley 7322 (late 14th c; *Index* 3411):

> The lif of this world
> Ys reuled with wynd,
> Wepinge, drede, and steriinge: [*MS. om.* drede
> With wind we blowun,
>   With wind we lassun;
> With weopinge we comen,
>   With weopinge we passun.
> With steriinge we byginnen,
>   With steriinge we enden;
> With drede we dwellen,
>   With drede we wenden.

147

82

Index 2025. MS. Harley 913 (e. 14th c.) contains an interesting group of poems (some of which are of Irish origin). See W. Heuser, *Die Kildare-Gedichte (Bonner Beiträge zur Angl.* xiv, 1904). At the end of the MS. there is a Latin version of the first two stanzas of this poem ('Lolla, lolla, parvule, cur fles tam amare?' etc.). Lullabies addressed by Mary to the Christ-child were common in the later 14th and 15th centuries; this poem is unique in being addressed to a human child, and in being a bleak *memento mori*. (See Woolf, p. 155.) The same idea is developed in a ME sermon (MS. Royal 18 B. xxiii) discussed by G. R. Owst, *Literature and Pulpit* (revised ed., 1961), p. 37, where the 'prophete of wrechednes' describes the cry of the weeping babe from a cottage door —'Welaway! why was I resceyved in anny womans barme?' (Cf. also ibid., pp. 533, 536.)

19–22. Cf. *CB XIV*, No. 42:

> The levedi Fortune is bothe frend and fo,
> Of pore che makit riche, of riche pore also;
> Che turneth wo al into wele, and wele al into wo,
> No triste no man to this wele, the whel it turnet so.

25–6. A traditional commonplace (cf. Heb. 11: 13, 1 Pet. 2: 11, etc.) given memorable expression by Egeus in the *Knight's Tale*:

> This world nys but a thurghfare ful of wo,
> And we been pilgrymes, passynge to and fro ...

29. *wo the worp Adam.* For the phrase, Carleton Brown compares 'wo him wes ywarpe yore' in *Midelerd for mon wes mad (CB XIII*, No. 75, l. 65). There was a traditional belief that men when born cried 'A!', the first letter of Adam's name (see Furnivall, EETS xv, p. 252).

31. *an uncuthe gest*: cf. *Index* 2067:

> Man ys dethys underlyng,
> Man ys a gest in hys dwellyng,
> Man ys a pylgrym in his pasyng.

83

Index 1402. MS. Add. 22283 (the 'Simeon MS.') (l. 14th c.) is very closely related to the Vernon MS. in the Bodleian Library, which contains the other known copy of the poem. On the relationship between the MSS. see K. Sajavaara, 'The Relationship of the Vernon and Simeon

MSS', *NM* lxviii (1967), 428–39, and *The M.E. Translations of Robert Grosseteste's Château d'amour* (Helsinki, 1967), pp. 101–27. (Cf. also Doyle, RF, pp. 328–41) This poem is one of a group of lyrics with refrains which the two MSS. share (see *CB XIV*, Nos. 95–120). It is a remarkable meditation on the human state, based on some passages of Ecclesiastes (especially chapter 1); it exhibits a pessimism, perhaps springing from the frequent 'scepticism' of contemporary philosophical thought, and the fideism which often accompanies it. On the poem see Fr. G. Sitwell, 'A Fourteenth-century English Poem on *Ecclesiastes*', *Dominican Studies*, iii (1950), 284–90, and Woolf, pp. 111–12.

12. *this worlde fareth as a fantasy*: cf. the quatrain pr. EETS viii, p. 85 (*Index* 190):

> All hyt is fantome that we withe fare
> And for othere mennes goode is all oure care;
> Alle come we hyder nakude and bare,
> Whenne we hethene passe is there no mare.

Cf. also what seems to be an expanded version of this in Horstmann, *Yorkshire Writers*, ii, pp. 457–8 (*Index* 189).

13 ff. Cf. Eccles. 1: 5 ff.
23. *as a gest*: cf. No. 82, l. 31.
25 ff. Cf. Eccles. 1: 4, 11.
49 ff. Cf. Eccles. 3: 19–21.

84

Index 4044. On MS. see No. 8(b). Above the English is written a Latin version, possibly its original:

> Cum sit gleba tibi turris
> Tuus puteus conclavis,
> Pellis et guttur album
> Erit cibus vermium.
> Quid habent tunc de proprio
> Hii monarchie lucro?

The ideas are commonplace, but the English lyric expresses them with sharpness and irony. Other verses of this type are usually much less successful. Cf. these lines (spoken by a dead man) in MS. Adv. 18.7.21 (*Index* 1210.5):

> Her sal I duellen, loken under ston;
> Her sal I duellen, joy is her non;
> Her sal I duellen, wermes to fede;
> Her sal I duellen, domes to abide.

On the ancient theme of the contrast between the smallness and meanness of the grave contrasted with the splendour of the dead man's life on earth, see Woolf, pp. 82–4. Cf. (among many examples) *CB XV*, No. 156:

· · · · · ·

> Quhen thow art ded and laid in layme,
>   And thi ribbis ar thi ruf tre,
> Thow art than brocht to thi lang hayme—
>   Adew al warldis dignite!

85

Index 4160. MS. Laud Misc. 23 (e. 15th c.) contains a number of English pieces. This ME version of the *Cur Mundus Militat* was extremely popular; it occurs in 11 MSS. (another version, *Index* 3475, is printed by Person p. 18). It is a jerky and halting version, although (as usual) the 'ubi sunt' passage is good. The Latin hymn remained popular after the Middle Ages. There is a good Elizabethan version in *The Paradyse of Daynty Devyses* (1576); the hymn, according to the Elizabethan editor, condemns 'the unstable felicitie of this wayfaring worlde'. Another version ('Why doth this world contend?') is found in Richard Verstegan's *Odes in Imitation of the Seaven Penitential Psalms* (1601), and was that used in Nicholas Ferrar's community at Little Gidding (see H. P. K. Skipton, *The Life and Times of Nicholas Ferrar* (London, 1907), pp. 109, 197–8).

13 ff. The 'ubi sunt' theme is frequently used in this type of 'mortality' literature. See the discussion by E. Gilson, 'De la Bible à François Villon', *Les Idées et les lettres* (Paris, 1932), pp. 9–30, 31–8. The list is sometimes one of the riches and splendours of life, sometimes of exemplary figures from the Bible, or classical or romantic literature, sometimes even including a famous contemporary who has recently been snatched away by death (*CB XIII*, No. 43, ll. 81–2, for instance, mentions 'Henry ure kyng'). See also Woolf, pp. 93–7, 106–19.

16. *duke Jonathas*: cf. 1 Sam. 14 f. It seems that the English poet either misread Lat. *dulcis* as *dux*, or used a MS. with the latter reading. The other ME version (*Index* 3475) has *swete Jonataas*.

18. *the riche man*: cf. Luke 16: 19–31, a favourite parable with medieval homilists.

26. *a shadewe*: Lat. 'Quam breve festum est haec mundi gloria / Ut umbra transiens sunt eius gaudia.' A separate translation of this stanza is found in Grimestone's preaching-book (*Index* 1262):

> Hou sort a feste it is the joyye of al this werd,
> Als the schadwe is of man in this midel-erd,

That often time withdrawith the blisse withouten ende,
And drivet man to helle to ben ther with the fende.

The image is a Biblical one (cf. Job 8: 9, 14: 2; Ps. 101 (Vg.): 12, 108: 23;
Eccles. 8: 13), and is frequently found in devotional literature. See also
G. V. Smithers, 'Two Typological Terms in the *Ancrene Riwle*', *MÆ*
xxxiv (1965), 126–8. The stock image is used vividly in a poem in the
Vernon MS. (*CB XIV*, No. 101, ll. 121–32):

> I have wist, sin I cuthe meen,   [speak
>   That children hath bi candel liht
> Heor schadewe on the wal isen,
>   And ronne therafter al the niht;
> Bisy aboute thei han ben
>   To cacchen hit with al heore miht,
> And whon thei cacchen hit best wolde wene,
>   Sannest hit schet out of heor siht;
> The schadewe cacchen thei ne miht,
>   For no lynes that thei couth lay. [*i.e.* as to catch birds
> This schadewe I may likne ariht
>   To this world and yusterday.

33. *wormys mete*: Lat. *esca vermium*, a common phrase in this type of
literature (cf. *cibus vermium* in No. 84, note). It is recalled in Mercutio's
grim jest 'they have made worms' meat of me' (*Romeo and Juliet*, III.
i. 104).

86

Two examples of a very popular series of lyrics, 'Earth upon earth'.
Forty-one MS. copies of the various versions are recorded; many are
edited, with a commentary, by Hilda Murray, *Erthe upon Erthe*, EETS
cxli (1911). They are based on the text 'memento homo quod cinis es et
in cinerem reverteris', which is used in the Ash Wednesday liturgy. See
Woolf, pp. 84–5.

(*a*) *Index* 3939. MS. Harley 2253 was probably written in the fourth
decade of the 14th century (see N. R. Ker's Introduction to the facsimile
(EETS cclv); it contains an important collection of English and Anglo-
Norman poems. This is an example of Murray's 'A-version'. Another,
longer, example is found in MS. Harley 913; a variant (*Index* 703) in
MS. Adv. 18.7.21, f. 87ᵛ (text Wilson, p. 27).

(*b*) *Index* 704; from MS. Egerton 1995 (*c.* 1430–50, the commonplace
book of William Gregory), is an example of Murray's 'B-version', an

expanded and rather weakened version, which is found in a number of MSS. dating from the 15th to the 17th century. In this MS., as in some others, the poem is preceded by the lines

> Memento homo quod cinis es et in cinerem reverteris
> Whenne lyfe ys moste lovyde, and dethe ys moste hatyde,
> Deth drawythe hys draught, and makythe man nakyde.

'Earth upon earth' remained popular for a very long time. There are versions, or echoes, of it in tombstone inscriptions until the 18th century, and some of its phrases seem to have become proverbial (cf. Peele's *Edward I*, sc. 24, 'An old said saw, earth must to earth', or the allusion in Shakespeare's Sonnet lxxiv, 'The earth can have but earth which is his due').

87

Index 4045. On MS. See No. 14 note. There are a number of versions of these curious mortality verses, usually known as the *Proprietates Mortis* (see *Index* 3998, 4033, 4076, 4047, 187, and the discussions by Woolf, pp. 78–82, 330–2, and Robbins, 'Signs of Death in ME', *Medieval Studies*, xxxii (1970), 282–98). The 'signs of death' found in ancient medical literature, e.g. the Hippocratic Prognostics, were turned to homiletic use in the Middle Ages. They are found as separate verses in early ME (see *CB XIII*, pp. 130, 220–2); there are echoes of the tradition in the Worcester Fragments of the *Address of the Soul to the Body*. Grimestone's preaching-book has some similar lines (*Index* 1220)

> *Homo in fine*
> His colour blaket
> His mirthe slaket
> His heved aket
> His bodi quaket . . .

Cf. Jeremy Taylor's *Holy Dying*, chapter 1:

Baldness is but a dressing to our funerals, the broker ornament of mourning, and of a person entered very far into the regions and possession of death; and we have many more of the same signification; gray hairs, rotten teeth, dim eyes, trembling joints, short breath, stiff limbs, wrinkled skin, short memory, decayed appetite.

The 'signs' survived in popular medical lore also. Cf. Oscar Lewis, *Life in a Mexican Village* (Urbana, 1951), p. 415: 'It is believed that when a person is about to die "his eyes go up and become whitish, his nose sharpens, his hands get cold and still, and his body becomes loose".' The idea is put succinctly in a tag in C.U.L. MS. Ii., 3.8, f. 84ᵛ:

> Wanne hol man is turned into half man,
> Thanne cometh deth faste:
> Than schal naut longe laste.

1. *thi nese scharpet*. This detail is found in some of the earlier versions (see *CB XIII*, pp. 221–2) and appears again in the description of Falstaff's death in *Henry V*, 'his nose was as sharp as any pen'.

7. Proverbial; cf. MS. Douce 52, f. 26 (in a collection of proverbs): 'Alle to late, alle to late / When deth is come to yate'.

88

Index 1387. A 15th-century English version of the Latin *Vado mori*, a poem found in MSS. of the 13th and 14th centuries (see W. F. Storck, *Zeitschrift für deutsche Philologie*, xlii (1910), 422–8), in which a series of human figures, arranged more or less in hierarchical order—king, pope, bishop, knight, physician, logician, etc.—all complain that they must 'go to die'. Each complaint consists of a single couplet, beginning and ending with the words *vado mori*, thus:

> Vado mori, rex sum, quid honor, quid gloria mundi?
> Est via mors hominis regia: vado mori.

> Vado mori, miles, belli certamine victor,
> Mortem non didici vincere: vado mori.

> Vado mori, logicus, aliis concludere novi;
> Conclusit breviter mors mihi: vado mori. . . .

The poem is clearly one of the antecedents of the *Dance of Death*, and, like it, is sometimes treated as an illustrated poem. All three of the 15th-century MS. copies of the English poem are accompanied by pictures: in B.M. MS. Add. 37049 a crude drawing shows skeletons with a spear behind each of the three figures; in B.M. MS. Stowe 39 a rather more handsome illustration shows the three figures confronted by a skeleton holding a spear (the three stanzas are placed above the figures of the victims, and in this version Death is also given a stanza); in Cotton Faustina a much more talented artist has treated the scene— the three victims are sensitively drawn, and show genuine sorrow in their expressions (they hold scrolls containing the verses, and there is no sign of a skeleton or a figure of Death).

10. *mare and dill*. This vague phrase completely loses the macabre force of the philosophical word *concludere*; the grim pun is found elsewhere in vernacular poetry, e.g. Henryson's *Three Deid Pollis*, l. 23, or Dunbar's *Lament for the Makars*, l. 39:

> . . . rethoris, logicianis, and theologgis,
> Thame helpis no conclusionis sle;
> *Timor mortis conturbat me.*

89

Index 769. MS. 15th c. The poem is also found in MS. Balliol 354. The last stanza appears separately in B.M. MS. Lansdowne 762 with the heading *epitaphium*. It was in fact sometimes used as an epitaph in the late 15th century. Examples are, or were, attested at St. Michael's Crooked Lane, St. Martin's Ludgate Hill, and at Romford, Northleach, Baldock, Royston, and Maldon (see Gray, 'A ME Epitaph', *NQ* ccvi (1961), 132–5). It is noticed by Wordsworth in one of his essays on epitaphs as 'a great favourite with our forefathers'. The poem is an example of the 'Farewell to the world' spoken by a dead or dying man who makes a brief lament *de contemptu mundi* (see *CB XIV*, No. 97, *CB XV*, Nos. 159, 160, etc.). It has a solemn dignity, handles the traditional themes confidently, and to some extent exploits the dramatic possibilities of the 'farewell' form (see Woolf, p. 323).

2. *arested*: a common image. Cf. Lydgate's translation of the French *Dance of Death*, where Death announces to the Constable (l. 137):

> It is my right to reste, and yow constreine
> With us to daunce, my maister Sir Constable.

It is used again in *Hamlet* (v. ii. 328–9), 'this fell sergeant Death / Is strict in his arrest'.

8. *a cheyre feyre*: 'A fair held in cherry-orchards for the sale of the fruit . . . often the scene of boisterous gaiety and licence. Formerly a frequent symbol of the shortness of life and the fleeting nature of its pleasures' (*OED*) (the cherry season lasts only a short time). Cf. *CB XIV*, No. 117, l. 85, *EEC*, No. 371 and note.

12. *chek-mate*: cf. *CB XV*, No. 151, l. 33 ('yit in a whyle thou schall be cheke-mate'), *Gesta Romanorum*, ed. H. Oesterley (Berlin, 1872), ch. 166, G. R. Owst, *Preaching in Medieval England*, p. 326.

21. *ane horne*: probably the trumpet with which Death is often

depicted in late medieval art and literature; possibly the last trumpet (1 Cor. 15: 52).

29. *the tide abidith no man*: the proverb is found elsewhere in medieval works. Cf. Lydgate's *Fall of Princes*, iii. 2801, or Death's words to Everyman (*Everyman*, 143). See Whiting, T 318.

90

Index 2414. By James Ryman (see No. 59 note).

91

Index 1254. MS. e. 16th c. Written in the margin, possibly by Thomas Lower, one of the owners. The same hand has written on f. 44ᵛ this verse:

> Whan shall relyfe reles my wo?
> Whan shall my lyfe be dethe be seste?
> Whan shall my happy hape be so
> That my pore harte may come to reste?

'Nowe cometh al ye' was called by Carleton Brown 'Death, the port or Peace' (*CB XV*, No. 164; cf. ibid., p. xxix, Woolf, p. 69). R. L. Greene has shown (*MLN*, lxix (1954), 307) that it is a stanza from Walton's 15th-century translation of Boethius, *De Consolatione Philosophiae* (it is copied in fact from the early 16th-century printed version of the work) and that its primary reference is to God. It is the beginning of metrum 10, Book III:

> Huc omnes pariter venite capti
> Quos fallax ligat improbis catenis
> Terrenas habitans libido mentes,
> Haec erit vobis requies laborum,
> Hic portus placida manens quiete,
> Hoc patens unum miseris asylum . . .

Chaucer's gloss clearly says 'This is to seyn, that ye that ben combryd and disseyvid with worldly affeccions, cometh now to this sovereyn good, that is God, that is refut to hem that wolen come to hym.' But, naturally enough, the idea of death is present also, and is emphasized by the images of 'rest' and of 'port'. Cicero (*De Senectute*, ch. 19) makes Cato compare the approach of death to the sight of land and to coming into harbour after a long voyage. The figure becomes common (cf. Harrington's 'Death is a porte wherby we passe to joye'). The humble,

even grateful, acceptance of death, which is so unlike the macabre spirit
of much of the 'mortality' writing of the late Middle Ages, is not
unknown in devotional literature, although it is uncommon. The idea
that after a holy life death is to be welcomed is sometimes found (see
CB XV, No. 163 and note). The learned poets could recall the Ciceronian
image: see the passage in Dante's *Convivio*, IV, c. xxviii, which describes
how the noble soul in her last age

returns to God, as to that port whence she departed when she came to
enter upon the sea of this life; she blesseth the voyage that she hath made,
because it hath been straight and good and without the bitterness of
tempest. And here be it known that, as Tully says in that *Of Old Age*,
'natural death is as it were our port and rest from our long voyage.' And
even as the good sailor, when he draws near the port, lowers his sails, and
gently with mild impulse enters into it, so ought we to lower the sails of
our worldly activities and turn to God with all our purpose and heart;
so that we may come to that port with all sweetness and all peace.
(tr. Wicksteed)

1. *Nowe cometh*: the reading of the MSS. of Walton's Boethius has
been restored (cf. also the Latin text and Chaucer's gloss quoted above).
Our copyist seems to have used Thomas Rychard's printed version,
which has the incorrect reading *Howe cometh*.

92

Index 233. The song of the angels in the *Pilgrimage of the Soul* (see No. 3
note) as the pilgrims enter heaven. It occurs at the beginning of Book II;
the pilgrims leave scrip and burden behind and pass through the curtain
after their angels:

and so also sone as thei were entrid withynne forth thei songen a song
withoute comparisoun more lusty than I had herd tofore, and though it
passe my witte and myn abilite forto counterfeten hit in verray trewthe
of lyknesse, yit somwhat as I can sympely reporte I shal here rehersen. . . .

37. *he*: presumably the body (*thei* (l.43): your individual bodies).

GLOSSARY

Except initially *y* is treated alphabetically as *i*. Words which are explained in the notes are omitted.

a, ever.
a, on, at.
abated, diminished, destroyed.
abeyist, pay for, redeem.
abit, remains.
abone, above.
aboughte, about, paid for, bought, redeemed.
abounde (*aj.*), plentiful, abundant.
abusion, falsehood, perversion.
acros, in the form of a cross, (?) with arms outspread.
adamauntt, adamant, loadstone, magnetite.
adyghte, adorned.
adreynt, drowned.
afered, afraid.
afor(e), aforn, before; **here aforn**, before this.
agayn, agene, ageyns, again(st), in return, back.
agoo (*p.p.*), gone.
ay(e), ever; ~ **and oo**, for ever and ever.
ayenis, against.
al, completely; ~ **and sum**, altogether.
algate, in any case.
alkyn, of all kinds.
allweilding, omnipotent.
almest, almost, well-nigh.
als, also, as.
alswa, also.
alther, of all.
amorwe, in the morning.
an, and; on.
and, if.
andled, face.
anon(ne), at once; ~**ryght** straightway.
antane, anthem, antiphon.

apere, appear.
araide, full evill ~, in a miserable state.
areride, raised.
arest, ceasing.
aryvage, arrival.
arn, are.
as, throw of one at dice (the lowest possible throw).
asautus, assaults.
asythe, reparation.
assayde, tried, experimented.
assignement, allotting; decision, determination.
astrout, sticking out.
aswounde, swooning, feeble.
at, at, from.
atte, at the.
attome, at home.
atwo, in two.
availe (*n.*), assistance, advantage.
avisement, advice, counsel.
awarde, custody.
aye, ayen(e), ayein, ayeyn, again, once more, back, against, contrary to.
ayens(t), against (47.4), compared with.
axist, askest.

bable, bauble, plaything.
baite, allurement, bait.
baldeth, becomes bold.
bale, sorrow, misery.
balett, song.
bar, bore.
barne, child.
barst, burst, broke.
be, bi, by, in.
be (*v.*), be; **beit, beth, ben(e), beoth** (*3 pl.pr.*), are; **beese** (*imp.*), be.

157

bedith, arrayed.

beerde, maiden.

beheest, promise.

beyen, buy.

beit, *see* be.

below (*v.*), laughed at, derided.

bem, pillar.

bemene, complain; (43.91) (?) complain, (?) intercede.

bemette, destined.

ben, *see* be.

beoth, *see* be.

bere (*n.*), (83.6) bier.

bere (*n.*), byre, cattle-stall.

bere (*v.*), bear; bere (*pa.t.*), bore.

beren, son.

beryd, buried.

beryng, birth.

besek, bisek, beseech; besout (*pa.t.*), besought.

beshrew, curse.

besynesse, activity, anxiety.

bespreynt, sprinkled.

best(e), beast, animal.

bet, bett(e) (*pa.t.*, *p.p.*), beat, beaten.

bete, amend.

beteche, biteche, commend, deliver.

beth, *see* be.

betoght, delivered.

beverech, drink.

bewepen, weep for.

bewte, beauty.

byd, bidde, pray, bid, command; beg.

byd(e), wait.

bidropped, bedewed.

byhalde, biheld, behold; bihild (*pa.t.*), beheld.

bihedde, guarded, protected.

biheve, (83.71) (*?3 sg.pr.sjv.*) may be necessary.

byhycte, promised.

bylde, (86(*b*).11) built.

bylde, (60.37) dwell.

binome, taken from.

birdyn, burden.

bisprad, covered.

byspreynd, besprinkled.

byssad, drenched.

bistedde, beset.

biswongen, beaten, scourged.

bytand, biting.

bythenche (*refl.*), consider.

bitwene (*adv.*), at intervals.

biwevid, covered, enveloped.

blaket, becomes pale.

ble(e), colour, complexion, appearance.

blede, bleed; bledis (*2 sg.pr.*); blet (*3 sg.pr.*); bledand (*pr.p.*), bleeding.

bleyc, pale.

blent, blinded.

blicht, joyful.

blisfulhede, joyfulness.

blyssit, blisced, blessed.

blithe (*aj.*), joyful, happy.

blithis (*v.*), gladdens.

blive, quickly.

blo(e), livid, blackish blue.

blowe (*v.*), ~ a bost, brag.

blw, blue.

bo, both.

bobbid, buffeted.

boet (*pa.t.*), beat.

boghen, bow, submit.

boght, bowhte, bought, redeemed.

boklyd, fastened with a buckle.

bolles, swells.

bondyn, bowndyn (*p.p.*), bound.

bone, request, petition.

bood (*pa.t.*), experienced.

boren, born.

boryd, pierced.

borwyng, borrowing.

bos, behoves, is necessary.

bo(o)st, boast, vaunt, menace, pomp.

bot(t), *see* but.

bote, remedy, relief, salvation.

botefull, bringing deliverance, able to rescue.

boun, make ready.

bounte, goodness, virtue.

bour, bowr, bower, bedchamber.

brayd, moment.

braunche, (60.51) offspring, child.

bredde, (63.18) was engendered, born.

breer, briar.

breme, fierce(ly).

brennyngly, fervently.

brent, kindled, on fire.

brest, break.

brewing, drink which has been brewed.
briht, bright.
britel, brokel, fragile.
brol, offspring, brat.
brouht, brout, brought.
burd, ought to.
burdoun, pilgrim's staff.
burnes, men, servants.
bus, (61.15) must.
but(e), bot(t), but, unless, without, except for; ~ **if,** unless.

caas, event, happening.
cacchen, catch.
campyoun, champion.
carfull, sorrowful.
cese, take possession of, seize.
chambre, bedchamber.
Chanaan, Canaan.
chapman, merchant.
charge, burden.
chasid, driven, pursued.
che, she.
cheevest, chiefest, pre-eminent.
cheyere, throne, chair.
cheld, shield.
chepyng, market, market-place.
che(e)re, cheir, cher (n.), demeanour, mood, appearance, gladness, joy. **cheres** (v.), makes cheerful, encourages.
chese, choose, take; **che(e)s** (pa.t.); **cheoseth** (3 sg.pr.).
cleped, clepedest, called.
clere, cleir (aj.), clear, pure, bright.
clere (v.), clear, make clear, purify.
clergye, clergy, clerkly skill, learning.
clypp(e), embrace.
clo, claw.
clos, helle ~, closed prison of hell.
clout, piece of cloth.
coldet, grows cold.
comberaunce, distress, annoyance, perplexity.
compile, put together, write.
conjoyned, united.
convenyent, appropriate, congruous.
converte, turn.
cors, body.
couth, knew how to, could.

coveitise, covetousness.
covent, company.
cover, recover, rescue.
covetynge, object of desire.
crake, crack, break.
Crestendam, Christendom.
crippe, see **skrippe.**
croce, crosce, cross.
crokes, hooks.
crope, head (of a plant).
crunyd, crowned.
cussyng, kissing.

daliaunce, delight, courtly pleasure.
damme, lady.
dawe, day.
ded(e), death; ~ **stunde,** pains of death; ~**ly** (aj.), mortal.
defaute, lack, want.
degre, manner, state, rank.
dey(e), deyyen, die.
deynte, delightful.
del (n.), part; **never a ~,** not at all.
dele (v.), divide; (43.92) have to do with.
deme, judge; **demed, demytt** (p.p.), judged, condemned.
departed, separated.
der(e), dyre (aj., adv.), dear, precious; dearly.
dere (v.), injure, harm.
dere (n.), deer.
derworthi, dereworthy, precious.
devyse, relate, describe.
devors, separation.
dill, (?) benumb; (?) silence, lull.
dim, dark, sombre.
dinet, (?) become deaf.
dyntes, blows.
dyre, see **dere.**
dyrk, dark.
discryve, describe.
disese, dissees, trouble, distress, misfortune; ~**ed,** distressed.
dissaite, deceit, concealment.
disseyvable, deceitful.
dissevere, part.
do, do, make, cause; **dois** (pl.pr.), **dos** (3 sg.pr.); **do** (p.p.), done; **doede** (pa.t.), did; ~**se upon,** put on.
dome, judgement.

dop, deep.
doun (*aj.*), dark, gloomy.
dowtte, fear.
dowve, dove.
draught, action of drawing a bow.
dreameth, make melody.
drede, **dreid**, fear.
drei, **drie**, suffer; **dreed** (*pa.t.*), suffered.
dreynte, drowned.
drerely, sorrowfully.
dreury, sweetheart.
drincst, **drinkest**, (29.28, 16) give to drink; **dronk** (29.27) (*pa.t.*), gave to drink.
droh, drew.
druye, dry.
dulles, blows.
dun, down.
dune, hill.
dunnet, grows dark.

eche, (13.3) same.
eyen(e), **ene**, eyes.
eysyl, vinegar.
elde, age.
eldren, elders.
elles, else.
enamelyd, adorned.
encheson(e), reason, cause.
encrece, **encreas**, increase.
enhawnce, elevate.
entent, intention, desire.
entere, entire, whole.
enterly, completely.
entreted, treated.
eorthe, earth.
e(e)r, before, previously.
erd(e), earth.
eren, ears.
erndie, intercede for.
ernemorwe, daybreak.
ernen, run.
ertow, art thou.
euch, each.
everichon, everyone.
exult, (39.2) (? *p.p.*) exalted, triumphantly joyful.

farly, marvellous.
favour, beauty.

felle, fierce; **fellest** (*splv.*), fiercest.
fe(e)nde, fiend, devil.
feyntt, (57.1) feigned.
fender, defender.
fere, **ferre**, far.
fere (*aj.*), healthy.
fere, **fer** (*n.*), companion; **in ~**, together, as well.
feste, feast.
fete, neat.
fyled, defiled.
fill, fell.
fyn(e) (*aj.*), pure, consummate; **make it ~**, bring it to consummation.
fyne (*n.*), end.
fisses, fish.
flagat, flask.
fle, fly.
fleme, put to flight.
fless, flesh.
flytt, **flitth**, fleeth.
fode, food.
fo(o)de, offspring, child.
fol, **foul**, wanton.
foldet, fails, falters.
folily, with folly.
fomen, foes.
fonden, tested, put to the proof.
fonding, temptation.
fonge (*p.p.*), seized, taken.
for, (60.66) (?) in reward for; **~ thine**, (34.13) (?) for thy part; **~ whome**, (51.47) on whose account.
forborne, weighed down.
fordo, destroy.
forewoundyd, wounded to death.
forgon, lose.
foryete, forget; **foryete(n)** (*p.p.*), forgotten.
foryeve, **foryef**, forgive.
forlete(n), lose, give up.
forlore, lost.
forte, **forto**, to.
forthi, therefore.
foules, birds.
fra, **fro**, from.
fre, generous, noble.
freelte, frailty.
frele, frail.
frere mynours, Franciscans.
fretid, gnawed, bitten into.

ful, full, foul.
fulsum, plentiful, bountiful.
funde, go.

gan(ne), gane, gone, did.
gef(f), geve, gif(f), gife, give.
generacions, generations, descendants, progeny.
gentill, noble, gracious.
gyfe, shackle, fetter.
gyn, begin.
glit, glides.
glore, glory.
god(e), goud, goode, gud, good, benefit: **the to ~,** for thy benefit.
gome, man.
gore, robe.
gostly, spiritual.
govern, rule, direct, guide.
grede(n), cry, call.
gref, hurt, pain.
gresse, herbage, leaves, herb.
grest, see gret.
gret, gryte, great, big; **grest** (83.20) (splv.), greatest.
grett, greeted.
greveth, grevyt, distresses.
grysliche, terribly.
grome, anger.
ground(e), grunde, earth, foundation, depths, root; **bringet me to ~,** casts me down; **on ~ grest** (83.20) (?) greatest on earth = the greatest that exists.

habbynge, having, possession.
hafdis, haddest.
hayld, pulled.
ham, them.
ha(y)me, home.
hap (n.), fortune.
hap(p) (v.), **me ~ ys** is my lot.
har, their.
hat, (11.51) am called.
hey, heigh, high.
heyed, see hiye.
hele (n.), health, prosperity, salvation.
hele(n) (v.), heal.
hem(e), them.
hende, gracious.
henge, hung.
henne, hence.

hent(e), caught, snatched, seized.
heo, they.
heor, their.
herbere, arbour.
herde, shepherd.
here, here (pron.), her, their.
heryen, praise.
hert(e), heart; **~-rote,** depths of the heart.
hete, hett, promised.
hethen, hence.
heved (n.), head.
heved (p.p.), raised.
hevede, had.
heven(e), hewyn, heaven; **~ king, ~ riche,** king, kingdom of heaven.
hext, highest.
hi (pron.), they.
hi(e) (aj.), high.
hyde, hidden.
h(i)ye, hasten; **heyed them,** hastened; **hyed** (p.p.), driven.
hyme, hymn.
hyng(e), hang, hung; **~and,** hanging.
hit, it.
ho, who.
hoem, hoere, them, their.
hol(e), holl (aj., adv.), whole, sound; wholly, entirely.
honden, hands.
hocle (n.), hole.
hope, (11.56) hop = dance.
hosyll, housel, communion.
hoso, whoso.
houres, canonical hours, offices.
hui, they.
hur(e), her.
hurld, thrust, shoved.
hwar, where.

ibor(en), born.
ic, ich, ik, I.
icheece, chosen, excellent.
icoren, chosen.
ideliche, fruitlessly, vainly.
idyght, arrayed, placed.
ido, done.
idut, closed.
ifere, together.
ifrore, frozen.
iyarkid, prepared.

ikest, arranged, ordained.
ilke, same.
ilkone, each, each one.
iloken, closed, locked.
ilore, lost.
imakid, made.
imperiall, (39.26, 69.12) (?) of the empyrean.
in (*n.*), lodging, home.
inliche, deep, heartfelt.
innome, taken.
innosable, not destructive.
intretid, treated, handled.
ipreved, proved.
is (*n.*), ice.
isame, together.
isen, seen.
istonge, istungen, pierced.
iswungen, beaten.
itake, committed.
itald, itold, considered, reckoned.
itent, stretched.
ivel (*adv.*), badly.
iwys, indeed, certainly; **mid ~,** certainly.

jangel, chatter.
jantilnesse, gracious behaviour.
Jewlye, Jewishly.
joyneth, join, follow.
joyng, delight.
juberte, peril.
Juery, Jews.
jurneis, days, journeys.

kan, know, be able to.
kar(e), care, trouble, sorrow.
kedde, showed.
ken (*n.*), kin, progeny.
kende, *see* **kinde.**
kene, sharp.
kenestol, kinestol, royal throne.
kenne (*v.*), know.
kest, cast, turned.
kinde (*n.*), nature; **kende** (1(*b*).3), race, kin; **kuynde** (83.126), (?) natural vitality, **~s,** (83.103, 104), created species, races.
kynde (*aj.*), natural, showing natural affection, naturally generous, kind.
kyndeli (*aj.*), natural, according to nature.

kynedom, kingdom, rule.
kithe, show.
knewe, knew, recognized.
knyttyth, fastens, draws together.
knokytt, beaten.
kuynde, *see* **kinde.**
kunredes, kindred, races, kin.

ladde, led.
layke, play, sport.
layme, loam.
langhyght, befits.
langyng, (43.29) (?*aj.*) longing.
langynge (*n.*), longing.
langis, me ~, I long.
lappe, fold of a garment.
lapped, wrapped.
largenesse, generosity.
lassun, decrease, fade.
lat(e), laten, let.
lathly, hatefully, terribly.
launche, branch.
lavedi, lady.
lawse, free.
leche, physician.
lef (*v.*), *see* **leve.**
lef(e) (*aj.*), dear, beloved.
leff (*n.*), leaf.
lele, loyal, true.
lemys, limbs.
lemys, rays.
lemman, lover, sweetheart.
lenger, longer.
lent, given.
leove, beloved.
ler(e), leren, teach, learn.
lese, lose; **les,** lost.
lesse, ~ and more, small and great.
lessun, reading, something to be learnt.
lete, (34.3) shed (tears).
lett, give up.
lettith, prevents.
leve, lef (*v.*), leave, give up, abandon, cease, leave off.
le(e)ve (*v.*), believe.
levedi(e), lady.
levene, flame.
levere, rather.
leveth, lives.
lib, live.
liche, like.

lichtnes, illuminates.
lyf(fe), life, creature.
lift, left.
liggus, lies.
lyghtand, illuminating.
likand, pleasing.
lykinge, pleasure, desire.
Lymbe, Limbo.
lyne, lineage.
lisse, tranquillity, peace, joy.
list (n.), pleasure, joy, delight.
list (v.), please.
lyt, little.
lithe, supple.
loffyng, loving.
loft, on ~, on high, aloft.
loke(n), look; ~ed ylle, (?) were in a bad state.
lordling, prince.
lore, teaching, doctrine, rule of behaviour.
lorn, lost.
loth, hateful.
louyng, praise.
loveliche, lovely.
lovered, louerd, lord.
lovien, love.
lovynge, (49.7) beloved one.
lowe (n.), love.
lowed, humbled.
lowse, loose.
luff, lufe (n., v.), love; ~er, lover.
luytel, little.
lull, ~id, lulled, soothed; ~ynge, soothing.
lust (v.), desire, wish; hym ~, it pleases him.
luther, wicked.

may, maid.
maiden-man, virgin.
maistrie, maystrye, mastery, domination, superior power; (43.37) (?) masterful, dominating behaviour (?) phr. = it is no hard thing.
make, mate, consort; ~les, peerless, without a mate.
mamelles, breasts.
manchipe, courtesy, humanity.
mar(r)e, destroy, (88.10) confuse, bewilder.

margarite, pearl.
markyd, set down, destined.
mat, (83.43) (?) mat, (?) form of mote = mote, atom, particle.
material, consisting of matter, physical, corporeal.
mede, reward.
mede, meadow.
medle, be concerned with.
mek, mekhe, meek.
mekyl, mekull, great.
mele, time.
memoryall, commemoration.
mende (n.), see mynde.
mende (v.), amend, restore.
mene, course.
menyhe, company.
ment, intended.
merciable, merciful.
meschief, misfortune.
mete, food, meat.
meve, agitate, discuss.
mych(e), much.
micti, mictu, could I, could you.
midelerd, earth.
mykel, mycull, great.
mylde(ly), myelde, mild, gentle, gently.
mylsfolnesse, mercy.
myn, mention, recall.
mynde, mende (n.), mind, memory.
mynde (v.), have mind, think upon, remember.
minde (aj.), present to one's thoughts.
myrour, mirror, example.
myrth, joy.
mys, misdeed(s), wrong; amiss.
myscheff, wickedness, misfortune.
mysese, misery.
mysse (v.), lack, be without, want, fail to attain, fail.
mo, more.
mode, mind.
molde, earth.
mon, man; ~kunde, mankind.
mo(o)ne, complaint, lament.
mor(e), more, greater.
mort, dead.
mortualite, mortality, mortal nature.
most (aj.), greatest, biggest.
most (n), must, juice of grapes.

GLOSSARY

mostou, must thou.
mot, mote(n), may.
mouht, moth.
mow(e), mown, may, must.
mowid, grimaced.
mund, *see* **mynde.**
murye (*aj., adv.*), merry, merrily.
murnind, mourning.

na, no.
nabbe, do not have.
nagt, *see* **nought.**
nay, this is no ~ it cannot be denied, it is certain.
naide, denied.
nam, took.
namely, especially.
narewe, narrowly, (?) keeping the legs close together.
narre, near(er).
naut, *see* **nought.**
nay, *see* **neye.**
ne, not, nor.
nede, nedis (*adv.*), of necessity.
neye, nay, near, close at hand.
nere, near.
nert, art not.
nese, nose.
newyne, name.
newyng, repeating.
ny, near.
nis, is not.
nobleye, nobility.
noyous, troublesome.
nome, name.
norse, nurse.
nost, not, do not know.
note, to ~, for the use of.
nouht, nowht, nout(t), nagt, naut, not, nought, nothing.
nouthe, now.
nuyyeth, vexes.
nurture, upbringing, training.
nutarst, (?) now for the first time.

o, one.
o, on; ~ blode, with blood.
occasion, cause, reason.
occe, ox's.
occupacion, business; control of affairs.

of(f), of, off, from; **~ blode** (32.25) = bloody.
offence, without ~, unblemished.
offes, office.
oght, owght, ought, at all, anything.
on(e), oon, a, one, alone; **al ~, by hyr ~,** alone.
onavysed, without warning.
onde, breath.
onece, onys, once.
onkende, unkind.
onsene, face.
onuppe, above.
op, up.
ore (*n.*), mercy.
osprynge, offspring.
other, othir, owther, other, or, either, whether; **it wolde be noon ~** it could not be helped.
ou, owe, ought.
ous, us.
owttrage (*v.*), break away.

pace, walking pace.
pacyens, patience.
pay (*n.*), satisfaction; **the devil to p~,** to please the devil.
palefrey, palfrey, saddle-horse.
pappe, breast.
Parais, Paradise.
par case, perchance.
parcyall, (?) to have a part, to share.
parfijt, perfect.
pasche, Paschal.
pavis, shield.
pees (*v.*), to make peaceful.
peynted, painted, feigned.
pere, peer, equal.
pety, *see* **pyte.**
pyghte, fixed, placed.
pykys, make trim, comb.
pine, torment.
pit, pit, abyss.
pyte, pety, pity, mercy, compassion.
place, (60.13) palace (cf. 43.21 *var.*).
play (*v.*), disport.
playne (*v.*), lament.
plates, silver coins.
plenere, plenerly (*adv.*), fully, completely, perfectly.
plentevous, bountiful, generous.

poyntes, particulars, qualities.
polist, polished.
pore, pouer(e), poor.
porful, poor.
porpure, purple.
porte, bearing.
portes, doors, gates.
precellyng, surpassing, pre-eminent.
prek, prykke, pierce, nail.
pres, crowd, mêlée.
prest (*aj., adv.*), quick(ly), eager(ly), readily.
preve, prove, test.
prime, the first hour.
pris(e), prys, worth, excellence, value; **bere the ~,** have pre-eminence; **ipreved on ~,** whose excellence has been proved, of tried excellence.
priulie, gallantly, with prowess, powerfully.
pryvely, privately, intimately.
privete, hidden purpose, secret wisdom.
processe, discourse.
promoteth, advances.
propyrte, property, attribute.
pursyvant, pursuivant (a junior heraldic officer), messenger.
purvaide, prepared, provided.
purvyaunce, providence.
put, pit.

quanne, qwan, qwen, when.
quell, kill, destroy, overcome.
quhame, quhome, whom.
quhilk, which, who.
quhill, while, until.
quhois, whose.
qui, why.
qwat, what.

rasid, torn, scratched.
rather, sooner, better; more quickly; **~ or,** rather than.
ratilet, rattle.
reason, (24.3) power of description.
rebounde, (64.46) (?) abound, overflow.
recche, care for; **ne ~ me nought** (47. 42), may I care nothing for; **roughte** (*pa.t.*), cared for.

recchelesse, heedless, negligent, unattentive.
recover, return, make one's way.
red, reed.
rede, counsel, plan; **wat sal me to ~,** what can I do?
redy, (43.67) ? willing, close at hand, ? prudent.
refourmed, restored.
reherse, relate.
relaxit, loosened, released.
reme, realm.
renne, run.
rentes, revenue.
res, rash, impulsive action.
reseyve, receive.
reuful, pitiful, sad.
reuled, directed, guided, ruled.
reuli, rewly, rulye, pitiful(ly).
reuthe, mercy, pity.
reve, rob, snatch from.
rewe, reu, have pity (on); **me ~th,** I pity.
ryal, royal.
ryfe, quickly, promptly.
ryg, back.
ryght, riht (*adv.*), precisely, indeed, right.
ryght, ryht (*n.*), right; **on ~,** rightly; **ne speke bote ~** (40.5), only speak what is just.
ryghtwos, righteous.
ryn(ne), run.
ripe, ripe, fitting.
rys, thicket.
ryve, plentiful, abundant.
rode, roud, cross.
rode, (21.2) face.
rody, ruddy, red.
rooten, (83.125) rot.
rosscheth, rush.
rote, (83.127) rotted.
rote, rute (*n.*), root.
roughte, *see* **recche.**
route, rowt(t)e, company.
ruf-tre, roof-beam.
rulye *see* **reuli.**
rutelet, rattle.

sa, so.
sad(de), shed.

sayh, saw.
saikles, innocent.
sal, salt, shall, shalt; **saltu,** you shall, you must.
salve, salve, ointment.
salvour, healer.
sannest, suddenly.
sare (*aj.*), grievous.
sare (*n.*), grief, distress, pain.
sarpe, sharp, bitter.
sate, (3.10) lay.
sawe, speech, discourse.
schal, shall, must.
schamefastnes, modesty.
scharpet, grows sharp.
schef, creature.
schelde, schilde, shyld, protect.
schent, shent, destroyed, injured, punished.
schet, vanishes.
schewid, shown, revealed.
schour, attack, conflict, throe.
schroud, garment.
schule(n), shall.
sclepie, sleepy.
scloe, slow.
scole, school.
se, so.
seche(n), seek.
see (*n.*), sea.
sege, seat, throne.
sey, (61.73) ? sigh, ? say.
seye (*pa.t.*), saw.
seyne, seen.
seke, sick.
selcowthe, exceedingly.
sely, blessed, innocent.
selli, seollich, strange, wondrous.
selve, the ~, (83.10) that very man.
sennewess, sinews.
sentence, opinion, judgement.
seo, seoth, see.
seollich, *see* selli.
sere (*aj.*), divers, various.
sere (*v.*), (83.73) (?) injure, wound, (?) blight.
seson, in good ~, at the proper time.
seste, ceased.
set, ~ not by, thought nothing of.
sete, sett, seat, throne.
sethyn, since.

sewe (*v.*), appeal, petition.
sewyngly, in succession.
shake, (3.5) (?) released, dislodged, (?) snatched.
shene, bright, glorious.
shennesse, humiliation.
shent, *see* schent.
shyld, *see* schelde.
shlou, slew.
shole, shall.
shome, shame.
shryfte, confession.
shrudde, clothed.
sich, syche, *see* sike.
syght(e), siht, sicht, sight; **in ~,** to look upon.
syhtyng, sighing.
sike, sigh.
siker, sure, secure, certain.
silit, sell.
synguler, unique, individual.
syt, (61.73) (?) grieve.
syth, since.
skyis, clouds.
skyll, reason, cleverness.
skyrte, kilt.
skrippe, scryppe, crippe, bag, wallet (esp. one carried by a pilgrim).
slake, lessen, mitigate.
slaver, spittle.
slawe, slain.
sle, slay.
sleye, slyye, skilful, prudent, wise.
sleuthe, sloth.
slycht, treachery.
slomoryng, slumber.
sloven, knave, rascal.
smert(e), painful.
sojurne, dwell.
sokyd, sucked.
solas, joy.
soldi, should I.
solemply, with great dignity.
son(e) (*adv.*), quickly.
sory, grievous.
sort (*aj.*), short.
sorte (*n.*), (?) destiny, (?) company.
sorwe, soru(e), sorrow.
sorwuel, sorrowful.
sotell, subtle, crafty.

soth, truth.
souelis, souls.
soughte, souht, soht, sowhte, sought, went to, came to, searched, investigated, (40.17) looked about.
soun, (83.59) speech.
soune, sun.
sour (n.), sour taste.
sownyng, swoon.
sped(e), succeed, prosper, fare, assist, send quickly, (57.91) comprehend.
spelle (v.), speak, describe.
spilen, destroy; spilt (pa.t.), destroyed.
splayd, spread.
springe-wel, spring, fountain.
spurnyd, stumbled, tripped.
ssal, ssalt, ssulen, shall, shalt, shall.
staleworthe, stalwart.
stall, seat of office, seat of honour.
stane, stone.
stanged, pierced.
stant, stands.
starket, grow stiff.
stede, place.
steigh, sthey, ascended.
stekyn, shut.
steriinge, (?) sorrow, perturbation.
stern, steren, sterre, star.
sterte, sprang, started.
sthey, see steigh.
stif, firm, valiant.
styfliche, boldly, strongly.
styghe (pa.t.), rose,
styye, rise.
stil, styll(e) (aj., adv.), quiet(ly).
stil (v.), still, quieten.
stilly, quiet(ly).
styngest, piercest.
stynten, stint, stunt, stop, cease.
stithe, strong, stern.
stont, stands.
stounde, time, hour.
stoure, battle.
stoute, strong.
strayned, stretched.
strayte, streit(e), straytly, tightly.
streme, stream, outflow; (10.15) beam of light.
strenth (v.), strengthen.
stronde, stream.
studes, places.

stunteth, stop, stay.
sturde, cruel.
suavite, sweetness.
suete, sweyt, sweet; swettist, sweetest.
suithe, very.
suld, should.
sullest, sellest.
sunen, sins.
surly, surely, in security.
swange, struck.
swappys, blows.
sweieth, make melody.
swerde, sword.
swete (v.), sweat.
swetes, makes sweet.
swiche, swylk, swilc, such.
swynke, toil.
swngen, beaten.
swote, sweet.

tabard, a loose garment with sleeves, made of coarse material.
tac, take.
taght, taught.
tayd, tied.
tayled, settled, arranged.
talde, told.
te, the.
tem, offspring.
temynge, child-bearing.
teren, tears.
tha, then.
the (v.), prosper.
thef, thief.
thench, thenk(en), think, remember.
theos, these.
thylke, that, that same.
thinge, for mannes ~, for man's sake.
thynk, me ~, it seems to me.
thirlis, pierces.
this, this, thus.
tho, those, these.
tho(o), then.
thocht, thought, meditation.
thoenne, then.
thof, though.
thole(n), suffer, wait; tholi, I suffer; tholed(e) (pa.t.), suffered.
thonke, think.
thor, there.

167

thorled, pierced.

thorou, thoru, thoruth, thoroth, thorwe, through.

thorw-out, throughout.

thos, these.

thou, thow, though.

thourhsoht, pierced.

thowghty, doughty.

thretid, menaced.

throh, coffin, grave.

throwe, moment.

thurgh, thurh, thwrth, through.

thurstungen, pierced through.

thuster, dark.

thwarted, countered, replied.

tyde, time.

tyght, purposed.

til(l), tyll, to.

tine, tiny.

t'is, to his.

to, to, too, as, (61.15) until.

to(o), two.

toc, took.

to-drawe, pulled apart.

toened, injured, afflicted.

to-gnawe, gnawed to pieces.

tokyns, signs.

tolles, draws.

toon, the ~, the one.

torent, torn to pieces.

tothir, the ~, the other.

tour, tower.

towchedyn, touched.

trace, (83.95) explore, search out (the mystery of).

trayturly, treacherously.

travaile, labour, hardship, journey.

tre, treo, tree, wood, cross.

treulofe, truelove.

treuthe, *see* **trowth.**

tryne, train, retinue.

trist, trust; **~u,** trust thou.

tryumphald, triumphant.

troddares, treaders.

trone, throne.

troubil, troublous, violent.

trow(e), trouwe, believe.

trowth, treuthe, truth, fidelity, troth.

trwe, true.

turuf, turf.

tuur, tower.

uche, each.

uchon, each one.

uel, will.

umul, humble.

uncuth, uncouthe, unknown, strange.

undervon, received.

unfayned, unfeigned(ly), sincere(ly).

unkyndnes, unkendenesse, unkindness, lack of natural affection.

unlaced, unfastened.

unlothfulnesse, innocence.

unthriftynesse, unworthiness, lack of success.

up, up, upon.

uprissing, rising, resurrection.

upsodoun, upside-down.

ur(e), our.

vayre, fair.

vedde, fed.

vendus, fiends.

veray, verey (*aj.,* *adv.*), true, truly.

vertu, virtue, power.

vesage, face.

vyht, fight.

visited, (3.20) came and comforted.

vo, foe, enemy.

voyde, set aside.

vokete, advocate.

volk, people.

vor, for.

voryet, forget.

vourty, forty.

vram, vrom, from.

wayleway, alas.

wailyeand, valiant.

wayn, waggon, cart.

waite, watch for, lie in wait, (43.52) (?) observe.

wald(e), would, wished.

wan, when.

wane (*v.*), won.

wanne, pale, leaden-coloured.

war (*a.*), vigilant, prudent; (*interj.*), beware; **~ li,** prudently, wisely.

wardly, worldly.

warkys, deeds.

warn, (11.29) summon.
warn, refuse.
wasse, wash.
wat, what.
waverynge, changing in intensity, sometimes strong, sometimes weak.
waxin, waxen, grow(n).
wedde, pledge.
wede, clothing, garment.
wel, (84.3) skin.
wel(e), well-being, joy, happiness; thou wost not ~ when thou hast done (25.12) ? = when you have finished (fondling your child), you feel sorrow (whereas I continually lament).
welawo, alas.
well, spring, fountain, well.
wend(e), go; is went, is turned.
wene, expect; wende (pa.t.), expected.
wepind, weeping.
wepistou, weepest thou.
werchs, worse.
werd, world.
were, (83.116) (state of) perplexity, doubt, distress.
werk, deed.
werne(n), refuse, restrain.
werreie, make war on, attack.
werris, wars.
wete (a.), wet.
wetes (v.), wets.
whan, (82.16) from where.
wher, where, whether; ~as, where.
whoder, whither, whether.
wycht, wiht, wight, person, creature.
wid, with.
wil, see wylle.
wyld (a.), unruly, self-willed, licentious.
wild (n.), (?) wilderness.
wylle, pleasure; wil (77(a).6), desire, appetite; wyth ~, joyously.
wilne, desire.
wymman, woman.
wyn(ne), wnne (n.), joy, pleasure, grace, bliss.
wynd (v.), ~ up, (?) raise.
wyne (v.), win.
wysse, direct.

wit, wyt, wyht, with, with, by.
wit (v.), blame.
wit(t) (n.), knowledge, wisdom.
wit(en), wyt (v.), know.
wite (v.), protect, guard, defend, tend.
witerly, assuredly.
wythuten, without.
wnde(s), see wondis.
wnne, see wyn(ne).
wnto, unto.
wochsave, vouchsafe.
wod(e), woode, savage, mad.
woh, sin, wrong, injury.
wol (adv.), well, very.
wol(le) (v.), wish, will.
wolawo, alas.
woliche, woefully.
won (aj.), pale, wan.
won (n.), hope.
won(e), wony (v.), dwell.
wonde (v.), shrink, flinch.
wondis, wnde(s), wounds.
wonyng-stede, dwelling-place.
wonne, when.
wonse, once.
worching, deeds.
word, wordle, worilde, world.
wore, were, had been.
worp, contrived, brought about.
worship, ~pyng, honour.
wost, knowest.
wot(e), know, knows.
woxen, grew, turned.
wrangys, wrongs.
wrangwysly, unjustly.
wrapped, ~ in wo, enveloped in misery.
wrathe (n., v.), anger.
wrech (aj.), wretched.
wreche (n.), vengeance.
wrethe, wrath.
wretyn, written.
wryed, accused.
wrynge, wine-press.

y, yc, I.
yaf, yave, gave.
yate, gate.
ybete, beaten.
ych, each, every.
ycoyntised, apparelled.

GLOSSARY

ydyht, arrayed.
ydo(n), done.
ydrawe, drawn.
yede, went.
yef, if.
yef (*v.*), *see* **yeve.**
yelde, gave up.
yeldyng, giving, payment.
yen, eyes.
yer(e), year.
yerne (*v.*), desire.
yernyng (*n.*), desire.
yeve, yef, yiff, give.
ygurd, girt.
yhoved, waited, lingered.
yye, eye.
yif, if.
yiff (*v.*), *see* **yeve.**

yyftes, gifts.
yit(t), yyit, yiet, yet.
ylich, like.
ymeind, mingled, drenched.
ynoh, enough.
yode, went.
yongeth, goes, advances.
yore, long since.
yove (*p.p.*), given.
ypreched, preached.
ysene, seen.
ysome, together.
ystongen, pierced.
ystreit, stretched.
ytake, taken.
ytrodded, trodden.
yvel (*aj.*, *adv.*), evil(ly), bad(ly).
yvuled, defiled.

LATIN WORDS AND PHRASES
OCCURRING IN THE LYRICS

ad missam garulantes, chattering at Mass.

ad puteum multum flentes, weeping, to the pit (of hell).

amen! amen! dicentes, saying amen! amen!

aurora consurgens, O dawn rising.

ave, hail.

ave, regina celorum, hail, Queen of Heaven.

columba mea, my dove.

Cristus natus est, Christ is born.

de te genitrice, by thee his mother.

Deo gracias, thanks be to God.

divina impedientes, (?) hindering divine things.

ecce, ancilla Domini, behold the handmaid of the Lord.

effecta, made.

ego, flos campy, I, the flower of the field.

electa, chosen.

Eva peccatrice, by sinful Eve.

favus distillans, dropping honey.

felix fecundata, joyful, made fruitful.

filia Syon, daughter of Sion.

funde preces ad filium, pour forth prayers to thy son.

gaudeamus, let us rejoice.

gloria in excelsis Deo, glory to God in the highest.

gratia divina, by divine grace.

in cruce, in the cross.

in luce, in the light.

inferni, of hell.

macula, stain.

mater honorata, honoured mother.

mater regis angelorum, mother of the king of the angels.

O Maria, flos virginum, O Mary, flower of virgins.

parens et puella, mother and maiden.

pari forma, in equal form = in one substance.

parvum quem lactasti, whom thou didst suckle as a baby.

pro salute fidelium, for the salvation of the faithful.

pulchra ut luna, beautiful as the moon.

que est ista, who is this?

quem meruisti portare, whom thou wast worthy to bear.

quia amore langueo, because I languish for love.

regina celi, queen of heaven.

regina celi, letare, rejoice, O queen of heaven.

requiem eternam, rest eternal.

res miranda, a thing to be marvelled at.

revertere, turn again.

rosa sine spina, rose without a thorn.

salutis, of deliverance, salvation.

sed prece deponentes, (?) prostrating yourselves, bowing down.

sic vana famulantes, talking of idle things in this way.

superni, of heaven.

surge, mea sponsa, rise up, my spouse

tam pia, so devoted.

tota pulchra es, thou art entirely beautiful.

transeamus, let us go on.

velud maris stella, as the star of the sea.

velud rosa vel lilium, as the rose or the lily.

veni coronaberis, come, thou shalt be crowned.

veni de Libano, come from Lebanon.

veni, electa mea, come, my chosen one.

veni in ortum meum, come into my garden.

ventre quem portasti, whom thou didst bear in thy womb.

virtutis, of virtue.

vox tua, thy voice.

INDEX OF FIRST LINES

INDEX OF FIRST LINES